The Sexy Vegan Kitchen: Culinary Adventures In Love & Sex

Aimee Christine Hughes

Aimee Christine Hughes

DEDICATION

This book is dedicated to all who choose to venture along the wondrous path to vibrant health, increased sexual energy and compassionate living.

To my dear friends, thank you for the love, laughs and bottomless glasses of red wine.

To my family, I wouldn't be writing this book without your continuous love and support.

To Tres, for the artistic inspiration, literary commiseration and sexy vegan explorations. Besos.

CONTENTS:

ACKNOWLEDGMENTS

Merci to all the lovely ladies and gents who have paved the vegan path for me. Thank you to the great tradition of yoga that has inspired me to live a life with greater awareness and compassion.

i

INTRODUCTION: HEAL THE PLANET, HEAL YOUR LOVE LIFE

During one chapter in my own life - the year of 2010, to be exact - I lived in a little bungalow a *pahoehoe's* throw away from Captain Cook's idyllic and infamous Kealakekua Bay. It was in this tropical paradise on the south Kona coast of Hawaii's Big Island where I began my own journey back to nature, swimming with yellow tang fish every morning, kayaking with the spinner dolphins and meandering lazily through the quaint Hawaiian neighborhood scented with plumeria flowers and teeming with birdsong.

By that time I had already begun eating a semi-vegan diet, but living in Hawaii and feeling the raw energy of Mother Nature was enough to 'wake me up,' so to speak. I had practiced yoga for over a decade at this point, and the idea of *ahimsa*, a Sanskrit term meaning, 'non-harming,' or 'non-violence,' never really sunk in until I lived on that beautifully lush island which heightened my awareness to the delicate balance of the Earth's eco-system.

Living in Hawaii meant eating a lot of raw, living foods because the climate is on average, a balmy 80 degrees year round and the fruit trees so abundant. Turning on a stove or baking in an oven became less and less the norm. By this happy accident I learned how good it felt to eat a largely raw, plant-based diet. Of course, the *mana* (energy) of the island, the clean air and regular exercise played a huge part, but I learned that what I ate, whether I was living in a tropical paradise or back in my Midwestern hometown, became the most fun and empowering way to take the reigns in regards to a healthy body, mind and spirit.

As many of us are aware, our precious eco-system is in need of some serious healing. As we approach a planetary population of 7 billion, it is clear that our current food system is unsustainable. The U.N. estimates that more than one in six people worldwide do not have access to enough clean water a day to ensure their basic needs are met. The Stockholm International Water Institute reports that 20 percent of the world's protein consumption is animal-based. If this statistic doesn't drop to 5 percent by 2050, a global food shortage crisis is unavoidable. The United States is the biggest culprit for this crisis. I remember reading a statistic once that claimed we would need seven planet Earths if everyone lived like us. Ouch!

The consequences of what we eat are far-reaching and the social implications of what we buy every day are infinite. Fortunately, our modern-day, industrial diet is on the decline. However, it is a very slow process. We can speed that process along by eating more plant-based, whole foods and less of the industrial stuff – refined sugars, refined flours, animals that have been injected with hormones and chemicals, genetically modified foods, etc. These aren't real foods. They are food-like products and most of them are laden with sugar.

In America today we eat, on average, over 20 teaspoons of sugar every day. This kind of sugar happy diet starves a healthy body and a healthy libido. Dairy is another food to examine if we want vibrant health. I love triple cream cheese on a fresh baguette and crepes overflowing with Nutella from street vendors in Paris as much as anyone. Having spent a lot of time in France, I have an emotional connection to these decadent foods. When I was a young student, traipsing through the streets of Paris on a shoestring, my daily bread consisted of cheap (albeit good) red wine, a warm baguette from the corner boulangerie, and a wheel of Brie from the neighborhood fromagerie.

Unfortunately, the processed dairy found on the shelves of our supermarkets today contain growth hormones and pesticides – even pus. If you really want dairy, can you find a local farm that produces dairy the way it used to be produced? If not, you're much better off without it. As a certified naturopath, I've been researching and writing articles for various magazines for nearly a decade now on the subject of health and wellness.

Endless studies show that at this time in history, when we are living an unnaturally indoor lifestyle, sitting behind a computer in a cubicle all day, then sitting in a car for an hour and coming home to eat food that is not really nourishing to the body, is literally starving us of our birthright to vibrant health. It's no wonder heart disease, diabetes, hypertension, obesity and various types of cancer are running rampant. The diet we want to strive for is one more akin to hunter-gatherer-gardeners – modern day hunter-gatherers who do moderate amounts of agriculture. Their diets are extremely high in nutrients while remaining low in calories – unlike the typical modern diet that has a very high amount of calories and a low amount of nutrition.

Alright, I know. Enough of the gloom and doom already. Right? Good. I believe you'll find that eating a largely plant-based diet brimming with colorful whole-foods is actually a lot of fun. (It's also easier on the pocketbook). Furthermore, it's essential for a better sex life! Yes, you heard me - a better sex life!

Food and love and sex are deliciously complex – delicate morsels of life – emerging from deep within the folds of our stories – past, present and future. What we eat and how we share those experiences is deeply personal. I write this cookbook in hopes that you will find a few recipes within, that become staples in the repertoire of your uniquely sexually-supportive food symphony.

Most of the recipes here focus on living foods – as in raw fruits and vegetables, although there are also warming soups and a few cozy baked goodies along the way. All recipes contain at least one of the foods I've termed 'sexy players.' The sexy players have been researched for their proven libido-enhancing properties.

I also use honey in a handful of the recipes. While honey is not vegan, I've included it because I do eat raw honey from time to time because I love the taste as much as its sexy string of nutrients. Feel free to substitute with agave syrup or yacon syrup if you wish.

Flirt with the recipes offered here. I'm no professionally trained chef and these recipes reflect that simple, beginner's approach. They are easy enough to throw together as is, or use as a guideline for inspiration to create your own original nibbles with love and sex in mind. Most of the ingredients included in these recipes are wild, superfoods that give us energy and an increased awareness of our bodies as sexual forces of nature! May this book bring a smile to your face and newfound energy beneath the sheets. Here's to radiant health and sexual bliss!

Tea for Two

Most recipes in this book are meant to serve two lovers. A few stray from this equation - like some of the soups and baked goodies - but you'll figure it all out as you journey pleasurably through your very own **sexy vegan kitchen**.

CHAPTER 1

THE SEXY PLAYERS & MALADJUSTED VILLAINS

Introducing, the Sexy Players

Acai Berry, the Siren

She is one of the healthiest little berries on the planet as well as one of the most seductive. Hailing from deep within the Amazon rainforest in Brazil, the captivating femme fatale of South America, she will lure you with her feminine antioxidant power and amino acid goodness. Her sexual prowess includes, but is not limited to: increasing blood circulation in the body, which contributes to a sex drive boost, especially in the male species. She promises increased sexual energy and optimal sexual performance.

Almonds, the Ideal Lovers

Hailing from the Mediterranean, almonds are the ideal lovers, seducing females with testosterone, which heightens their male mortal's potency, and L-arginine, which enhances their man's erections. They are an ancient aphrodisiac nut depicted in artwork as far back as 3,000 B.C. Almonds are also an excellent source of vitamin E, a super sexy nutrient, as well as B vitamins and high-quality protein. The ideal lovers provide our bodies with the trace minerals, selenium and zinc, essential for sexual and reproductive health. Their seductive powers lie in the olfactory realm as well, inducing passion in the female mortal with their intoxicating aroma.

Banana, the Natural

Bananas transport our souls to far-flung tropical paradises, where our biological urges dominate. They contain bromelain, which increases libido and helps men suffering from impotence. Their potassium increases our orgasm muscles. In various regions of Central America, the sap from the red banana tree is drunk as an amorous elixir. Thus, the naturally phallic banana will always reign supreme in our quest for sensual and sexual well-being.

Cacao, the Pleasure Seeker

Chocolate in its pure form, cacao, feeds the largest sex organ in our bodies – our minds. This bon vivant releases chemicals that give us a natural high and the same endorphins ignited by sex. Cacao's magnesium is responsible for hormone production, while its zinc assists in fertility and reproductive health for both men and women. A couple of super sexy chemicals, phenethylamine and anandamide, are known for that fuzzy feeling associated with falling en amour. The pleasure seeker also increases serotonin, enhancing sexual desire and responsiveness, while increasing sensitivity to even the slightest caress.

Celery, the Trickster

This libidinous vegetable is a master seducer for sending its object mixed signals. First impressions are deceiving. There's nothing externally sexy about a plain ol' stalk of celery. However, behind the unassuming façade, lies apigenin, a tricky little substance that dilates blood vessels and stimulates the flow of blood to you-know-where … It also increases pheromone levels in a man's sweat, making him even more attractive to his mate. Madame Pompadour wasn't joking when she waxed poetic, "if women only knew what celery does to a man, they would travel from Paris to Rome to get it."

Chia, the Warrior

The chia warrior is a tiny, ancient seed, derived from the Mayan word, *chiabaan*, which means 'strengthening,' and is quickly becoming a staple for the modern sexual warrior. In pre-Columbian times, chia seeds were a large part of the Mayan and Aztec diets. They contain over sixty percent omega-3 fatty acids – more than any other plant on Earth. The chia warrior's treasure trove of protein, fiber, calcium, magnesium, B vitamins, iron, boron, zinc and antioxidants make these morsels of sexual vitality a necessity in any sexual warrior's pantry.

Citrus, Perfumado Sexuelle

Citrus fruits are the ultimate sexual perfume and their wealth of vitamin C is a potent libido booster that keeps our sex glands lubricated and flowing with prana. Citrus fruits increase sperm count and keep our juices vital. Some say these fruits make our private parts smell even better. Think pink grapefruit, Kaffir limes and Mandarin oranges. Keep a bowl of lemons on your kitchen table, or better yet, move to the Mediterranean and plant yourself a lemon tree.

Date, the Dandy

Oozing with amino acids to support a healthy sex drive, dates are succulent and sexy. Like any proper dandy, they are ambiguously masculine *and* feminine, reveling in their ability to take on whatever role is required at a given moment. The dandy also has the means to restore sexual drive, support endurance and promote overall sexual vitality.

Leafy Greens, the Stars

Leafy greens purify your blood and make it flow to all the right places. They are rich in vitamin E which catalyzes the production of sex hormones. Their manganese facilitates the production of estrogen while zinc encourages sperm production. Leafy greens double your nutrient load while remaining extremely low in calories. If you've got extra pounds mellowing out your sex drive, leafy greens such as kale can help you lose pounds and maintain a sexy body. Additionally, kale is high in protein, making it the true star of stars.

Maca, the Natural Viagra

Throw out your little blue pills and bow to the natural Viagra instead. Birthed in the high altitudes of the Peruvian Andes, maca is packed with B vitamins, calcium and amino acids. It has the ability to increase stamina, reduce fatigue and enhance male and female libido. Love bonus: maca is essential to keep on hand if you are a post-menopausal femme desirous of a boost in the boudoir.

Oats & Other Whole Grains, the Charmers

That morning bowl of oats - you know, the one that seduces you with its comfort and warmth in the cold, cold months - is high in zinc, and zinc is one of the most important nutrients for great sex because it increases testosterone. Testosterone increases sexual desire in both men and women. Whole grains provide our loving bodies with more of that good L-arginine - the stuff that eases mediocrity in your blood vessels and staves off erectile dysfunction. So, go ahead. Get that water boiling on the stove and add a cup of charming oats (quinoa, brown rice or barley will do, too) and give your heart life and sex life a daily dose of good, clean love.

Nutritional Yeast, the Charismatic

Providing the body with a healthy fix of nutritional yeast means giving it a powerful shot of magnesium, zinc, iron, phosphorus, chromium, selenium, amino acids, protein, biotin, folic acid and B12. Nutritional yeast is the only plant source for B12 and you can get your daily dose in just one tablespoon. These nutrients help support a sense of sexual self-confidence, sexual energy, and contentment – all essential characteristics of the charismatic lover. Read on to learn how to eat the illusive edible.

Immature love says, I love you because I need you. Mature love says, I need you because I love you.

- Eric Fromm

Sea Veggies, Goin' Deep

Sea vegetables are high in vitamins B1 and B2, which help produce sex hormones. Their manganese, iodine and selenium effect mood and metabolism in a good, good way. This is important because if you're not in the mood and your metabolism is sluggish, your sex life might be on the weebly-wobbly side as well. Sea veggies also contain our sexy nutrient, vitamin E, which regulates the function of sex glands while battling free radicals in the sperm membrane.

Strawberries, the Coquettes

Strawberries are brimming with antioxidants that boost blood flow to the sex organs. The delicate little 'heart nipples' boast high levels of zinc, a sexual superstar of a nutrient that helps a woman's body prepare itself for sex. It also governs the testosterone needed in a man for optimal sperm production.

Sexy, Sexy Spices, Mystical Lovers

Exotic, erotic, enigmatic spices are aphrodisiacs from distant lands. Chili peppers mimic the state of arousal, while cinnamon has been known to simultaneously bite *and* kiss. Saffron is the queen of spices – rich and luscious, while cardamom was used by Cleopatra in her seduction of Marc Antony. Research proves that our sex lives get spiced up by eating lots of spices. Follow Cleopatra's lead and become your own alchemist of spicy seduction.

Tomatoes, Voluptuous Love Apples

Tomatoes are high in vitamins A and C, making them potent immune boosters and free-radical fighters. Tomatoes are laden with lycopene, a powerful libido-enhancer for both men and women. Often referred to as the 'love apple,' the mere scent of them has been shown to increase penile blood flow by 5%. So, take a bite out of the crimson symbol of love and passion and take to the sheets. You won't be disappointed.

Vanilla, Lover Exotique

The scent of vanilla is on one hand, sexy and erotic, on the other, sweet and innocent. Since the time of the Aztecs, vanilla has increased lust among both men and women with its intoxicating aroma and exotic flavor. Studies have shown the scent of vanilla to arouse men - so ladies, why not rub your love regions with real vanilla bean? Vanilla is also a mild nerve stimulant, which enhances sexual sensation.

Maladjusted Villains, the Anti-Players

White Sugar and Other White Foods

These villains have absolutely no sexy nutrients in them. They are the refined sugars, cakes, breads and pastries. Artificial foods, like candies, snack crackers and sodas - yipes! These foods are the anti-players, tempting you with their addictive properties. So, don't be fooled! These guys will rob you of your sexual energy, leaving you feeling dull and disagreeable. White sugar spikes your blood sugar which decreases testosterone levels. You can satisfy your sweet tooth with natural sweeteners. Ever bitten into a Medjool date? Sexy and scrumptious.

Trans Fats

These guys are really bad for cardiovascular health, which is directly related to sexual health. Stay away from potato chips and crackers, buttery spreads, packaged foods, soup cups and Ramen noodles, fast foods, frozen dinners, baked goods from the supermarket bakery, candy, breakfast cereals and most supermarket salad dressings. Without good circulation, the penis has a hard time responding to much of anything. Avoid fatty meats and refined carbohydrates, as these foods are counterproductive to sufficient circulation. Men who suffer from erectile dysfunction usually have a cardiovascular issue. Eating heart-healthy foods means eating sex-healthy foods. Makes sense, non? Oui!

Excessive Canned Foods

Most canned foods contain a lining of BPA, an industrial chemical toxic to humans. Studies have shown the villain to have a detrimental effect on male libido, so head to the bulk section of your natural food store to stock up on beans, grains, nuts, seeds, dried fruits and legumes.

Excess Alcohol and Nicotine

Too many distilled spirits dull the sexual spirits. They also shrink the testes and evoke impotence. Nicotine contracts penile blood vessels while encouraging artherosclerotic plaque to form in them. Sexy? Mais, non!

A Send-Off For Our Sexual Odyssey

Love is blind, they say; sex is impervious to reason and mocks the power of all philosophers. But in fact, a person's sexual choice is the result and sum of their fundamental convictions. Tell me what a person finds sexually attractive and I will tell you their entire philosophy of life. Show me the person they sleep with and I will tell you their valuation of themselves. No matter what corruption they're taught about the virtue of selflessness, sex is the most profoundly selfish of all acts, an act which they cannot perform for any motive but their own enjoyment - just try to think of performing it in a spirit of selfless charity! - an act which is not possible in self-abasement, only in self-exultation, only on the confidence of being desired and being worthy of desire. It is an act that forces them to stand naked in spirit, as well as in body, and accept their real ego as their standard of value. They will always be attracted to the person who reflects their deepest vision of themselves, the person whose surrender permits them to experience - or to fake - a sense of self-esteem .. Love is our response to our highest values - and can be nothing else.

- Ayn Rand

CHAPTER 2

SUMPTUOUS SMOOTHIES, JUICES & SHAKES

Ancient Roman Beet Elixir

Ancient Romans regarded the juice of the beetroot to be a potent aphrodisiac.

Sexy players: leafy greens, celery & sexy spices

2 large beets, quartered
2 apples, quartered & cored
2 cups kale leaves
2 celery stalks
2-inch hunk o' ginger root

Juice all ingredients and stir to combine flavors. Pour into two glasses & sip with pleasure. (This is a standard morning juice to be enjoyed with coffee or tea upon waking. Easily digestible so you can drink up and then go back to bed and get busy!)

He who defends love will be secure. – Lao Tzu

Incan Imperial Maca Elixir

Want to perform like an Incan imperial warrior? Add maca powder to your juices and smoothies and let the King of Peruvian aphrodisiacs get to work!

Sexy players: citrus, dates & maca

4 cups raw carrot juice
juice of 2 grapefruits
1/3 cup hemp seeds
2 Medjool dates, seeded
2 t maca powder

Juice carrots. Blend carrot juice and remaining ingredients. Sip slowly & mindfully.

A purpose of human life, no matter who is controlling it, is to love whoever is around to be loved.

- Kurt Vonnegut

Vitamin C Libido Booster

Smoothies and juices heavy in citrus are really great for both the male and female libido. In fact, vitamin E (our sexy little nutrient) actually needs the help of vitamin C to carry out its work. The two vitamins work together to enhance our sexual drive.

Sexy players: citrus & sexy spices

10 carrots

3 oranges, peeled

2 lemons, peeled

2-inch hunk o' ginger root

6 mint sprigs + 2 extra for garnish (optional)

Place all ingredients in your juicer and pour into two glasses. Garnish with mint sprigs. Kiss & Sip!

Love is a canvas furnished by nature and embroidered by imagination.

- Voltaire

Kama Sutra Carrot Juice

Nutmeg has long been prized as an aphrodisiac by Arabs, Greeks, Hindus and Romans. Even the Kama Sutra speaks of the spice in its ancient pages of wisdom. According to Ayurveda, India's ancient healing system, nutmeg is considered to be an even stronger aphrodisiac than other sexy spices.

Sexy players: almonds, vanilla & sexy spices

4 cups carrot juice
1 cup almond milk
2 t pure vanilla extract
1 t ground nutmeg

Juice carrots.
Transfer carrot juice to a blender with remaining ingredients. Blend well and pour into two glasses. Bless the drink with a kiss and sip with delight.

Love is an intensification of life.

- Thomas Merton

Brazilian Femme Fatale Smoothie

This acai elixir is packed with nutrients to support your body, mind and spirit...sex organs, too!

Sexy players: acai, strawberries, bananas, dates, vanilla, maca, sexy spices

1 (3 1/2 -ounce) package Sambazon frozen Acai, 1 cup frozen strawberries, 1 cup frozen pineapple chunks, 1 banana, 2 T fresh ginger root, chopped, 2 T unsweetened shredded coconut, 1 T raw sunflower seeds, 1 T raw cashews, 1 T flaxseeds, 3 Medjool dates, seeded and torn into pieces, stevia, to taste, 1 t pure vanilla extract, 1 t maca powder, dash of cinnamon, 2 cups water, 1 cup ice.

Let all ingredients reside in your blender for a short time. Blend thoroughly. Serve your baby. Sip mindfully & with great pleasure.

**And did you get what
you wanted from this life, even so?
I did.
And what did you want?
To call myself beloved, to feel myself
beloved on the earth.**

- Raymond Carver

Lusty Libido Banana Smoothie

Sometimes, less is truly more. Great pleasure lies in creating something beautiful with less.

Sexy players: bananas, almonds, sexy spices

> **2-3 frozen bananas**
>
> **¼ cup raw almond butter**
>
> **2 T raw honey**
>
> **¼ t ground cinnamon**
>
> **3 cups water**

Blend all ingredients until smooth. Enjoy for breakfast, an afternoon pick-me up, or as a healthy dessert.

Sex strengthens the immune system. Orgasms release hormones beneficial to immunity. DHEA is one of them. It fights against colds and flu.

The Sexual Powerhouse

You simply can't go wrong with this one. It's packed with nutrients essential to a healthy sex life and a healthy life, in general.

Sexy players: avocado, bananas, chia

> **1 ripe avocado, peeled and pitted**

> **2 frozen bananas**

> **½ cup frozen blueberries**

> **1 cup cranberry juice**

> **1 cup coconut milk**

> **2 t chia seeds, soaked in ½ cup water**

Soak chia seeds for at least 30 minutes. Place all ingredients, including the chia gel in a blender and blend until creamy. Pour into two glasses. Sip slowly. Go back to the sheets.

A study by Queens University in Belfast suggested that having sex three or more times a week reduces the risk of heart attack or stroke in men by half.

The Dandy's Morning Drop of Love

Treat your baby to this special treat in the morning and see your squabbles slip away.

Sexy players: almonds, dates, vanilla, sexy spices

1/2 cup raw almond butter

3 cups carrot juice

8 dates, pitted and soaked in 2 cups water

½ t pure vanilla extract

1/8 t cinnamon

Soak dates for at least 30 minutes. Place all ingredients in your blender, including date soak water. Blend. Pour. Drink. Kiss. Allow nature to take its course.

Love and sex are things that give life some value, some zest. Miserable as flesh and blood is, it's still the best you can get.

- Unknown

The Tropical Tease

Add pumpkin seeds to your smoothies and salads for an added libido boost. They are high in zinc, which is important for preventing testosterone deficiency in men. For women, they enhance sex drive as well as vaginal lubrication.

Sexy players: whole grains, bananas, dates, vanilla, sexy spices

½ cup spelt flakes, 1 frozen banana, 1 cup frozen pineapple chunks, 2 T raw pumpkin seeds, 2 T raw sunflower seeds, 2 t flaxseeds, 4 Medjool dates, soaked in 2 cups water, 1 t pure vanilla extract, ½ t pure coconut extract (optional), 1 T maca powder, ½ t cinnamon, 1 cup ice.

After dates have soaked for at least 30 minutes, remove pits and place the dates and the date soak water in your blender. Add in all ingredients and blend until smooth.

Love is composed of a single soul inhabiting two bodies.

-Aristotle

Blueberry Seduction

Brazil nuts are always a useful addition to any smoothie as they are one of the few plant-based sources of selenium, a powerful antioxidant mineral essential for male sex drive and potency.

Sexy players: leafy greens, vanilla, sexy spices

> 1 cup organic frozen blueberries
> ¾ cup collard greens
> 2 T ground flaxseeds
> 2 Brazil nuts
> 1/2 t pure vanilla extract
> 1/4 t ground cinnamon
> 1/4 t ground ginger
> 2 cups water
> stevia powder, to taste

Blend. Pour. Sip.

The only law is the law of desire.

— Cyril Collard

The Garden of Eden Dessert Shake

Remember, the potassium and B vitamins in bananas are vital for sex hormone production!

Sexy players: bananas, almonds, chia, maca, vanilla

3 frozen bananas, 2 T raw almond butter, 4 t coconut oil, 2 T dried, unsweetened coconut, ¼ cup chia gel (create chia gel by soaking 2 T chia seeds in 1 cup water for at least 30 minutes), 1 t maca powder, ½ t pure vanilla extract, ½ t stevia powder, 2 cups water.

Place all ingredients in blender and push necessary buttons. Careful not to push buttons of partner. This has been known to create messy situations and at times dampening sex drive. Not to worry. There's always a time and place for make up sex!

All colors are the lovers of their opposites

- W. H. Auden

Smoothie Amore

Almond butter, cacao, bananas, vanilla … this is one sassy, sexy creation!

Sexy players: almonds, cacao, bananas, vanilla

6 T raw almond butter, 4 T raw cacao powder, 2 frozen bananas, ½ t pure vanilla extract, ½ t stevia powder, 2 cups water.

Place all ingredients in a blender and blend until lusciously creamy. Pour into two chilled glasses and sip sensuously.

Sex contains all, bodies, souls

Meanings, proofs, purities, delicacies, results,

Promulgations,

Songs, commands, health, pride, the maternal

Mystery, the seminal milk,

All hopes, benefactions, bestowals, all the

Passions, loves, beauties,

Delights of the Earth.

-     Walt Whitman

Starring, the Strawberry Date Shake

This drink is sultry, sexy and smooth ... not unlike your sweetheart.

Sexy players: leafy greens, almonds, bananas, strawberries, vanilla, dates

2 cups leafy greens, 4 Medjool dates, pitted and soaked in 2 cups water, 2 cups almond milk, 2 frozen bananas, 2 cups frozen strawberries, preferably organic, 2 T raw almond butter, 2 T flaxseeds, 1 T coconut oil, ½ t pure vanilla extract.

Soak dates in water for at least 30 minutes. Place all ingredients in your blender (including date soak water) and combine until smooth. Pour into two chilled glasses & toast your paramour.

Sometimes sex fantasies and sex toys replace what's really important - authentic, emotional connection. These aspects of sex certainly have their time and place, but are merely one piece of the pie.

Green God/Goddess Smoothie

Rule of thumb: generally, anything green is good for your sex life.

Sexy players: avocado, leafy greens, bananas

1/2 an avocado, 2-3 handfuls spinach leaves, 1 cucumber, peeled & roughly chopped, 2 frozen bananas, 2 cups water, pinch of stevia powder.

Place all ingredients in a high-speed blender and blend away! Pour into two glasses.

A good sex life not only makes you look and feel younger, it will also help you live longer.

Goin' Deep, A Spirulina Smoothie

Derived from the spirulina plant, this green powder contains over 100 nutrients. Packed with protein, all the B vitamins, minerals such as iron, potassium, magnesium, calcium, zinc and all the essential amino acids of a complete protein, spirulina is truly an essential staple in the **sexy vegan kitchen**.

Sexy players: bananas, sea veggies, almonds, vanilla, sexy spices

> 2 frozen bananas
> 1 T spirulina powder
> 2 Brazil nuts
> 4 hazelnuts
> 1 T almonds
> 1/4 t pure vanilla extract
> 1/4 t ground cinnamon
> 2 cups water
> pinch of stevia powder

Blend all ingredients until smooth.

Where there is great love, there are always miracles. 					**- Willa Cather**

Spiced Tantra Shake

Sometimes a little spice up above is all you need to spice things up down below.

Sexy players: bananas, almonds, sexy spices

> 3 frozen bananas
>
> ¼ cup raw almond butter
>
> ¼ cup fresh ginger root, chopped
>
> 1 T raw honey
>
> 1 t ground cardamom
>
> ½ t ground cloves
>
> ¼ t ground pepper
>
> 3 cups water

Blend. Sip. Jump your baby's bones.

Love must be learned, and learned again and again; there is no end to it.

- Katherine Ann Porter

The Pleasure-Seeker

This one's so luscious, you may want to save it as a dessert after an evening lovemaking session. After all, everything tastes sweeter after sex.

Sexy players: almonds, cacao, vanilla, dates, sexy spices

¼ **cup raw almond butter**

1/8 **cup raw cacao powder**

3 **cups frozen cherries**

1/2 **t pure vanilla extract**

3 **Medjool dates, pitted**

¼ **t ground cinnamon**

3 **cups water**

Place all ingredients in your blender. Blend until all ingredients have combined to form two rich and delicious smoothies.

Love involves a peculiar unfathomable combination of understanding and misunderstanding.

- Diane Arbus

Sweet & Innocent Strawberry Shortcake Smoothie

This sweet smoothie will naturally satisfy your lover's sweet tooth. Enjoy as a light dessert.

Sexy players: strawberries, citrus, vanilla, dates

3 cups frozen strawberries

1/2 t grated lemon rind

1 t pure vanilla extract

3 Medjool dates, seeded and torn into pieces

1/2 cup raw cashews

2 cups water

1/2 t stevia powder

Place all ingredients in a high-speed blender and combine well.

Caressing, cuddling, kissing ... these are equally as important as sex. If we focus only on the act of sex, it can become mechanical rather than spontaneous.

The Siren's Song

Every ingredient in this super-sexy smoothie is a known player in our quest for sexual fitness. Together, they create one of the best aphrodisiac smoothies on the planet.

Sexy players: acai, bananas, maca, dates, sexy spices, almonds

> **1 packet Sambazon frozen acai, 2 frozen bananas, 1 cup frozen blueberries, 1 T maca powder, 1 T acai powder, 1 T flaxseeds, 1 T coconut oil, 2 T date crumbles, dash of cinnamon, ¼ cup raw almond butter, 3 cups water.**

Place ingredients in your blender. Blend. Pour. Enjoy!

Peruvian Warrior Smoothie

This super sensual breakfast smoothie, with it's sweet and creamy demeanor could be mistaken for a dreamy dessert. It's up to you - or your baby. Compromise is always key.

Sexy players: bananas, cacao, maca, vanilla

3 frozen bananas

¼ cup raw peanut butter

2 T cacao powder

2 T maca powder

½ t pure vanilla extract

3 cups water

Blend all these libido-enhancing babies in your blender until lusciously creamy.

Being deeply loved by someone gives you strength, while loving someone deeply gives you courage.

- Lao Tzu

School Girl Fantasy

Creating rice milk from scratch is incredibly satisfying for your love organs!

Sexy players: dates, bananas, whole grains, chia, vanilla

> **6 dates, pitted and soaked in one cup water, 2 cups frozen, organic blueberries, 2 cups frozen banana, 2 cups homemade rice milk (store-bought if need be), 2 t ground flaxseed, 2 T chia seeds, soaked in 1 cup water for 30 min. or longer, ½ t pure vanilla extract.**

Blend all ingredients, including date-soak water until smooth. For homemade rice milk, cook 1 cup long-grain brown rice in 8 cups water. You'll cover the rice with water and bring to a boil. Then let simmer for a few hours until it reaches a pudding-like consistency. In batches, you'll blend the pudding and then strain it through a fine mesh strainer. Store in mason jars or other containers. Making nut milks from scratch is addictive and satisfying, and of course it's way better for your sex life than store-bought counterparts!

CHAPTER 3

SCINTILLATING SALADS

Vigorous Vinaigrette of Pistachio

Those leafy greens, our star players, will take
center stage in the middle of the day. A big salad
with all your favorite veggies, nuts, legumes, herbs
and spices is one of the best meals you can
munch on for lunch to ensure you get all your
essential sexy nutrients.

Sexy players: citrus, sexy spices, leafy greens

> **1/8 cup lemon juice**
> **1 T raw honey**
> **1 t ground coriander**
> **1/2 t ground cumin**
> **1/2 t sea salt**
> **1/2 t olive oil**
> **1/2 cup shelled pistachios,**
> **chopped**
> **1/4 cup water**

Blend all ingredients in a blender or food
processor and dress a big leafy green salad.

Sexual Prowess Acai Vinaigrette

Salads can become monotonous without exotic dressings to mix them with. Because lovers love novelty this vinaigrette is just what the doctor ordered.

Sexy players: acai, leafy greens

¼ cup acai juice, 2 T raw apple cider vinegar, 2 T tahini, 2 cloves garlic, ¼ cup extra-virgin olive oil, sea salt, to taste, black pepper, to taste.

Whisk all ingredients together and toss with your favorite mix of leafy greens and raw veggies.

I was born with an enormous need for affection, and a terrible need to give it.

- Audrey Hepburn

Hail Caesar: a Creamy, Dreamy Dressing

You and your baby will love this one. It's thick and creamy and tastes soulfully fresh.

Sexy players: almonds, citrus, nutritional yeast, dates, sea veggies, celery, leafy greens

¼ cup raw almond butter, juice of 1 lemon, 2 T nutritional yeast, 2 pitted Medjool dates, chopped, ¼ t kelp granules, 1 stalk celery, chopped, pinch sea salt, pinch black pepper, ¼ cup water, maybe a bit more, romaine lettuce & your favorite mix of raw veggies, nutritional yeast for topping.

Blend all ingredients (except the last two) in your blender until creamy. Serve over romaine lettuce and any other veggies you like.

The one thing we can never get enough of is love. And the one thing we never give enough is love.

- Henry Miller

Cupid's Asian Dressing

Another favorite of soulful lovers, this dressing may quickly become a staple in your midday repertoire.

Sexy players: almonds, dates, citrus, celery, sexy spices, leafy greens

> ¼ cup raw almond butter, 2 T date crumbles, juice of 1 lemon, zest of 1 lemon, 1 clove garlic, minced, 1 jalapeno, seeded & chopped, 1 t apple cider vinegar, 1 t soy sauce or nama shoyu, 1 celery stalk, chopped, 1 t wasabi powder, 2 T water, ¼ t turmeric, sea salt, ground pepper, to taste.

Place all ingredients in a blender and blend until rich and creamy. Serve over your favorite salad greens and/or raw veggies. Sprinkle with sliced almonds.

Pleasure is the object, duty and goal of all rational creatures.

- Voltaire

Mood-Boosting Nori Avocado Salad

There's nothing better than a dish you can whip up in a matter of minutes - leaves you more time to take your man (or woman) for a whirl.

Sexy Players: sea veggies, avocado, citrus

> **6 sheets nori, torn into pieces**
>
> **2 avocados, peeled, pitted and cut into cubes**
>
> **juice of 2 limes**
>
> **sea salt, to taste**

> Combine all ingredients in a large bowl. Serve in two smaller bowls. Enjoy with a warm cup of sake.

Those following a balanced-vegan diet will naturally be slimmer and more confident in their naked bodies.

Sassy, Spicy Mandarin Salad

You simply can't go wrong with a sweet and spicy salad.

Sexy players: citrus, dates, almonds, sexy spices

3 mandarins, peeled and segmented
1 mandarin, juiced
4 dates, seeded and chopped
1 T finely chopped red onion
12 almonds, toasted and chopped
1/4 t ground cinnamon
1/8 t ground cardamom
1/8 t ground cumin
1/8 t cayenne pepper

Juice 1 mandarin and set aside. Peel and segment 3 mandarins, chop onion and set aside. In a large serving bowl, combine juice, spices, dates, onions and almonds. Add mandarin chunks to the bowl and toss to combine.

Greater sexual activity in men helps reduce the risk of prostate cancer.

Libidinous Citrus Broccoli Salad

Broccoli is great for your man's libido due to its compound, Indole-3- carbinol, which reduces estrogen levels. If he needs a boost feed him this nutrient-rich salad and you may be taken pleasantly by surprise!

Sexy player: citrus

1 head broccoli, cut into bite-sized pieces, 2 cups chopped cabbage, ½ cup shredded carrots, 2 oranges, peeled and segmented, 1 cup fresh cilantro leaves, chopped, 2 T lemon juice, 2 T raw honey, 1 T orange zest, sea salt, to taste, ground black pepper, to taste, ½ cup olive oil.

Place all chopped veggies & fruit in a large bowl. Whisk together cilantro, lemon juice, honey, orange zest, sea salt and ground black pepper in a small bowl. Pour in the olive oil and whisk further. Combine dressing with veggies and serve.

A woman knows the face of the man she loves as the sailor knows the open sea.

- Honore de Balzac

Pheromone's Celery Salad

Garbanzo beans are sexy sources of protein. Adequate amounts of protein will give you the energy to sustain a healthy sex drive.

Sexy players: celery, citrus, dates, sexy spices

8 celery stalks, chopped, 1 ½ cups garbanzo beans, 6 large garlic-stuffed green olives, chopped, 1 cup parsley leaves, 3 Medjool dates, pitted and sliced, 2 T tahini, juice of ½ a lemon, pinch of turmeric, pinch of cayenne, pinch of cumin, sea salt, to taste, black pepper, to taste, splash of water.

Place chopped celery, garbanzo beans, olives, parsley and dates in a large bowl. In a smaller bowl whisk together remaining ingredients. Coat salad with dressing. Enjoy!

Love is the same as life, except you feel sexier.

- Judith Viorst

Aristotle's Lament

Reportedly, Aristotle advised Alexander the Great to forbid his soldiers from drinking mint tea during campaign times. No libidinous distractions, boys.

Sexy players: citrus

2 grapefruits, peeled and divided into segments, 2 oranges, peeled and divided into segments, juice of 2 limes, 1/4 cup raw cashews, 4 T fresh mint leaves, minced, sea salt, to taste.

Combine all ingredients in a large bowl. Serve in two smaller bowls with a bit of baguette smeared with coconut oil & honey.

More sex creates more testosterone, which has been found to reduce the risk of heart disease and decrease depressive tendencies.

Pluto's Celery Seducer

The ancient Romans dedicated celery to Pluto, their 'God of Sex.'

Sexy players: celery, citrus, almonds, sexy spices

2 ½ cups celery, sliced thin

juice of ½ a lemon

1/3 cup raw almond butter

½ a jalapeno, seeded & minced

1 t rice vinegar

1 t soy sauce or nama shoyu

1 t pure maple syrup

2 T water

sea salt and black pepper, to taste

Place sliced celery in a serving bowl. Combine the remaining ingredients in a blender. Coat celery with dressing. Serve in two bowls. Enjoy!

The Trickster's Spiceful Seduction

Chili peppers heat things up in the bedroom because they are ripe with capsaicin, a feel-good endorphin-releasing brain chemical.

Sexy players: celery, citrus, sexy spices

4 cups chopped celery, 2 ½ cups blue corn tortilla chips, crushed, ½ cup tahini, juice of 2 limes, 3 cloves crushed garlic, 1 large jalapeno pepper, seeded & minced, ½ cup water, sea salt, to taste, black pepper, to taste.

Place celery and tortilla chips in a large serving bowl. Combine remaining ingredients to make a dressing. Toss dressing with celery and tortilla chips.

Fancy lovers never last.

- Maxine Hong Kingston

Eros' Kale Salad with Cauliflower "Rice"

Substituting cauliflower for actual rice is a great way to incorporate more sexy nutrients into a midday snack.

Sexy players: leafy greens, avocado, citrus, almonds, sexy spices

7-8 cups kale leaves, chopped, 1 ripe avocado, pitted, peeled and cubed, juice of 2 lemons, 1/3 cup extra-virgin olive oil, 1 t sea salt, ½ cup sliced almonds, 1 head of cauliflower, roughly chopped, juice of 1 lime, 1 T coconut oil, 1 t chili powder, 1 t ginger root, chopped, 1 T raw honey, pinch sea salt, pinch ground black pepper, lime zest, for topping.

In a large bowl, combine kale, avocado, lemon juice, olive oil, 1 t sea salt and almonds. Set aside. Zest the lime. In a food processor, process lime juice, cauliflower, coconut oil, chili powder, ginger and honey. Add the cauliflower mash to the kale salad and stir to combine. Season with sea salt and black pepper and top with lime zest.

Sexy Kale with Avocado-Chia Dressing

You really can't get much sexier than a kale/chia/avocado trifecta!

Sexy players: avocado, chia, sexy spices, leafy greens

1 ripe avocado, peeled & seeded, 1/8 cup chia gel (soak 2 T chia seeds in 1 cup water for at least 30 minutes), ¼ cup tahini, 2 t soy sauce or nama shoyu, 2 t pure maple syrup, 2 cloves garlic, chopped, ½ t cumin, dash of cayenne pepper, 5 cups kale, cleaned and chopped, ¼ cup carrot, grated.

Combine the first eight ingredients in your blender to make a dressing. Place kale and carrots in a large serving bowl. Coat with dressing and serve.

To love another you have to undertake some fragment of their destiny.

- Quentin Crisp

An Ode to Coconut Oil ~

Coconut oil, the extra-virgin, unrefined variety - is an essential staple in the sexy vegan kitchen. Its uses are virtually endless and its health benefits are too. Books have been written on the subject, so here I'll stick to ours: SEX! As a natural lubricant, coconut oil is my favorite. It is effective without interrupting the vagina's natural flora. A little goes a long way, so that tub you purchase will last a long, long while - which is fine, because coconut oil has a nearly interminable shelf life.

> Coconut oil gives the body an immediate energy boost, so you may wish to add it to a smoothie before sex. For an even more potent energy boost, mix a tablespoon of coconut oil with a tablespoon of soaked chia seeds.

Massages are lovely ways to relax, while boosting the immune system and fostering intimacy. Coconut oil by itself is a very nice massage oil. Anytime you cook with oil, coconut oil is a safe bet due to its high smoking point. Ladies - regular application of coconut oil has been known to banish cellulite! Invest in a tub of extra-virgin, unrefined coconut oil. You won't be disappointed.

Come-Hither Kale & Romaine Chopped Salad

Simple, seductive kale – always a sexy vegan standby!

Sexy players: leafy greens, citrus

4 cups raw kale leaves, chopped, 3 cups romaine lettuce, chopped, juice of 1 orange, 1 t + 1 T extra-virgin olive oil, 1 apple, cored and chopped, 3/4 cup red onion, chopped, black pepper, to taste, 1 T white balsamic vinegar, 1/4 t Herbamare seasoning, handful of mixed nuts, handful dried cranberries.

Place kale in a large bowl and mix with 2 t of the orange juice and 1 t of olive oil. Massage kale and let sit until it wilts. Add lettuce, apple and onion. Add the T of olive oil, vinegar, remaining orange juice, pepper and Herbamare. Combine thoroughly, top with cranberries and mixed nuts & serve immediately.

What is irritating about love is that it is a crime that requires an accomplice.

- Charles Baudelaire

The Perfumed Garden Delight

Pine nuts enhance fertility with their zinc content and have been revered for their loving properties since the time ancient Roman soldiers ate them while marching into battle. An ancient Arab love manual, 'The Perfumed Garden,' prescribed them to increase a man's sexual vigor.

Sexy players: leafy greens, citrus, sexy spices

5 cups raw kale, torn into small pieces
2 apples, sliced thin
1/4 cup red onion, sliced thin
1 t soy sauce or nama shoyu
1 T lemon juice
1 T toasted sesame oil
1/4 t cayenne pepper
2 t pure maple syrup
2 T sesame seeds
3 T pine nuts

Place kale, apples and onions in a large serving bowl. Whisk soy sauce, lemon juice, sesame oil, cayenne and maple syrup in a small bowl. Coat salad with dressing, sprinkle sesame seeds throughout and top with pine nuts.

Sensual Sesame Nori Salad Squares

Rich in sexy nutrients and low in calories - perfect for lovers!

Sexy players: sea veggies, sexy spices

1 cup carrots, chopped, 1 cup cucumbers, peeled and chopped, 1 cup pea shoots, chopped, 2 nori sheets, cut into several squares, 1 T rice vinegar, 1 T soy sauce or nama shoyu, 2 t agave nectar, 2 T toasted sesame oil, dash of chili powder, 2 T sesame seeds, toasted.

In a small bowl, whisk together dressing ingredients - vinegar, soy sauce, agave, sesame oil and chili powder. Set aside. Chop veggies and set aside. Toast sesame seeds. Cut nori into squares and place a handful of veggies on top. Drizzle each square with dressing & sesame seeds.

Be patient and savor the sexual energy between you and your partner. Today, direct less of your attention towards the outcome of orgasm. Rather, enjoy the slow journey of feeling and simply being together – in whatever form it takes.

Serendipity Spinach Apple Salad

There's more than one reason Popeye ate so much spinach!

Sexy players: leafy greens, citrus, sexy spices

> 1 apple, cored & chopped
> 3 cups spinach leaves, chopped
> 1 shallot, minced
> 2 T lemon juice
> 1 T fresh basil, chopped
> 1 t agave nectar
> 1 T extra-virgin olive oil
> salt, pepper, cinnamon, to taste
> 1-2 T pistachios, chopped

Combine spinach, apples and shallots in a bowl.
In another bowl, whisk together the remaining dressing ingredients. Drizzle dressing over salad and top with pistachios.

The way to love anything, is to realize it might be lost.

- G. K. Chesterton

Soulful Cucumber Slaw with Cashew Dressing

Cucumbers are considered to be an aphrodisiac for women because they heighten our olfactory senses.

Sexy players: citrus, celery

1/2 cup raw cashews
1/2 cup extra-virgin olive oil
4-5 cloves garlic, chopped
juice of 1 lemon
sea salt, to taste
1 cup shredded carrots
1 cup chopped cucumber
3/4 cup celery, sliced thin
1/2 cup raisins
ground black pepper, to taste

To make the dressing, blend cashews, olive oil, garlic, sea salt and lemon in a high-speed blender or food processor. In a large bowl, combine remaining ingredients and mix with dressing. Season with pepper.

We cannot really love anybody with whom we never laugh.

- Agnes Repplier

Island Paradise Spinach Salad

The flavors of the islands will have you shedding your clothes and getting back to do as nature intended ...

Sexy players: leafy greens, citrus, sexy spices

8 cups fresh spinach leaves
1/2 cup red onion, thinly sliced
1/4 cup scallions, minced
1 radish, sliced thin
1 cup chopped ripe mango
1/2 cup unsweetened coconut shreds, toasted
1/2 cup roasted and salted cashews
juice of 1 lime
1 t agave nectar
1 t Dijon mustard
1/4 t cumin
pinch of cayenne pepper
2 T olive oil
pinch of sea salt
pinch of ground black pepper

In a large serving bowl, toss spinach, onion, scallions, radish, mango, coconut and cashews. In a small bowl, combine remaining ingredients to make a dressing. Pour dressing over salad and coat evenly. Enjoy with an equally light tropical drink!

Libido-Enhancing Mango Salad with Peanut Sauce

Mangoes are an outstanding source of vitamin C, vital for thriving sex organs.

Sexy players: celery, leafy greens

2 ripe mangoes, peeled, seeded and sliced, 1 green bell pepper, cut into thin slices, 2 celery stalks, cut into thin 1-inch slices, 1/3 cup red onion, diced, 2 cloves garlic, crushed, 2 T rice vinegar, 2 T raw peanut butter, 1 1/2 t agave nectar, 1 t soy sauce or nama shoyu, splash of water, ground pepper, to taste, 4 cups romaine lettuce.

In a small bowl combine vinegar, peanut butter, agave, soy sauce and water until you reach a desired consistency. Place remaining ingredients in a large serving bowl. Toss with peanut dressing & season with pepper.

I conceived at least one great love in my life, of which I was always the object.

- Albert Camus

The Enticing Edamame

The basil in this salad increases blood flow to sex organs and has been known to drive us all wild with its lascivious scent. Apparently, basil oil was used by Mediterranean prostitutes to lure their men into the bedroom.

Sexy players: almonds, citrus, sexy spices

> 2 cups edamame, shelled
> 1 1/2 cups cherry tomatoes, halved
> 3/4 cup cucumber, chopped
> 1/2 cup basil leaves, chopped
> 1/2 cup cilantro leaves, chopped
> 2 cloves garlic, pressed
> 1/4 cup slivered almonds
> juice of 1 lime
> zest of 1 lime
> 1 T extra-virgin olive oil
> 1 t white balsamic vinegar
> salt and pepper, to taste
> raw honey or agave for drizzling

For the dressing, place lime juice, zest, vinegar, olive oil, salt and pepper in a bowl. Whisk well. In another large bowl, combine remaining ingredients. Drizzle honey or agave over salad. Toss salad with dressing and serve.

Crazy, Creamy Corn-Avocado-Cabbage Salad

An avocado a day may just keep the sex doctor away. If you feel like it, top this salad with slices from a whole avocado. The more folic acid, potassium and vitamin B6, the better!

Sexy players: avocado, sexy spices

3 cups corn
1 avocado, peeled, pitted and chopped
1/8 cup Vegenaise (a vegan version of mayo found in health food stores)
1 cup red cabbage, chopped
sea salt and ground pepper, to taste
crushed red pepper flakes, to taste
your favorite hot sauce, to taste
1/8 cup raisins, (optional)

Combine all ingredients in a large serving bowl. Adjust seasoning to taste.

The deepest truths bloom only from the deepest love.

- Heinrich Heine

The Jealous Jicama Noodle Salad & Her Spicy Tahini Sauce

Jicama hails from Central and South America. An excellent source of vitamins C, E and the minerals potassium, copper, iron and magnesium, it's also low in calories and contains more soluble fiber than most vegetables.

Sexy players: citrus, sexy spices

**2 cups thinly sliced jicama
1 cup mung bean sprouts
1/8 cup scallions, chopped
1/8 cup tahini
1/8 cup soy sauce or nama shoyu
1/8 cup lemon juice
1 T pure maple syrup
1/4 t crushed red pepper flakes
splash of water**

Blend tahini, soy sauce, lemon juice, maple syrup, red pepper flakes and water. Set aside. If you own a spiralizer, you can weave the jicama into "noodle" shapes. Place all veggies in a large serving bowl and serve with dressing on the side, or toss dressing into salad, if you wish.

Concubine's Cucumber-Nori Salad

Sea veggies such as nori, kelp, wakame, spirulina, kombu and arame have been eaten for over 10,000 years. They are great supporters of your adrenal glands. When your adrenals are balanced, love energy flows freely.

Sexy players: sea veggies, sexy spices, citrus

1/2 of a nori sheet, 1 cucumber, peeled, seeded and sliced thin, 1/8 cup green onions, diced, 1/8 cup carrots, sliced thin, 1 t ginger root, chopped, juice of 1/2 a lime, 1 t toasted sesame oil, 1 t rice vinegar, 1 t soy sauce or nama shoyu, 1/4 t red pepper flakes, sea salt, to taste.

Cut nori into thin strips and let them sit in a bowl of warm water. Place the cucumbers, green onions, carrots and ginger root in a serving bowl. In another bowl combine the lime juice, sesame oil, vinegar, soy sauce and red pepper flakes. Pour dressing over veggies and mix well. Drain the seaweed and add to salad. Season with salt and serve whenever you wish.

Love has nothing to do with what you are expecting to get – only with what you are expecting to give – which is everything.

-Katherine Hepburn

Slinky Kelp Salad

Kelp noodles are made from super-natural raw kelp hailing from the deep depths of Mother Earth's vast blue sea. They're preserved in a naturally derived salt that comes from seaweed.

Sexy players: sea veggies, sexy spices, citrus

> 1 (12 - oz.) package kelp noodles
> 1 cup carrots, chopped
> 4 scallions, sliced thin
> 1/8 cup onion, chopped
> 1 t ginger root, minced
> 1 t jalapeno pepper, seeded, minced
> 1 t toasted sesame oil
> 1 T rice wine vinegar
> 1 1/2 t soy sauce or shoyu
> juice of 1/2 lime
> pinch of red pepper flakes

Drain kelp and pat with a paper towel. Place in large serving bowl. Add carrots, scallions, onions, ginger and jalapeno pepper. Mix dressing ingredients (sesame oil, vinegar, soy sauce, lime juice and red pepper flakes) in a small bowl. Coat salad with dressing and serve.

Wistful Walnut-Pear Salad

Walnuts are excellent sources of omega - 3's, which support your brain. The brain is our largest sex organ - so eat up!

Sexy players: dates, leafy greens

2 pears, cut into bite-sized pieces
1/4 cup walnuts, halved and toasted over the stove
2 dates, pitted & chopped fine
2 cups salad greens of your choice
2 T balsamic vinegar
1 T Dijon mustard
sea salt, to taste
ground black pepper, to taste

In a small bowl, whisk the vinegar, mustard, salt and pepper together. Toss greens, pears, walnuts and dates in a large serving bowl. Mix in the dressing or serve on the side. Bon appétit!

Love is an act of endless forgiveness, a tender look which becomes a habit.

- Peter Ustinov

The Naughty Pomelo

What is a pomelo, you ask? Why, an ancestor of our grapefruit, but much bigger, with thicker skin and perhaps more potency. The Chinese have been known on occasion, to boil a pomelo's skin and leaves in order to prepare a ceremonial bath that repels evil. If you and/or your lover have been naughty, you may wish to consider doing the same.

Sexy players: leafy greens, avocado, citrus

> **2 cups romaine lettuce, chopped, 1 avocado, seeded, peeled and cubed, 1 pomelo or grapefruit, peeled and cubed, 1/4 cup red onion, sliced, juice of 1 lime, 1 T soy sauce or nama shoyu, 1 T extra-virgin olive oil, sea salt, to taste, ground black pepper, to taste.**

On two plates place the lettuce, then top with avocado and pomelo or grapefruit chunks, alternating for color. Scatter with onions. In a small bowl combine lime juice, soy sauce, olive oil, salt and pepper. Drizzle the dressing over your colorful salad and serve.

> **Of all forms of caution, caution in love is perhaps the most fatal to true happiness.**
> **- Bertrand Russell**

Captain Corelli's Loving Kale Salad

Kale is one of the most nutrient-rich food sources on the planet. So go ahead, temper that nutrition overload with a shot or two of Ouzo. If not, a bottle of antiquitous Retsina will do!

Sexy players: leafy greens, sexy spices, citrus

> 1 head kale, chopped, 1 cup red bell pepper, diced, 1/2 cup green bell pepper, diced, 1 cup red onion, chopped, 3/4 cup Kalamata olives, halved,
> 10 pepperoncini, seeded and chopped.

For the dressing:

4 small cloves garlic, chopped, juice of 1 lemon, 1/4 cup virgin olive oil, 2 T red wine vinegar, 1/2 t dried oregano, sea salt and ground pepper, to taste.

Combine all salad ingredients in a large bowl and toss with the dressing. Serve in two bowls. Enjoy!

Chains do not hold a marriage together. It is threads, hundreds of tiny threads which sew people together through the years.

- Simone Signoret

Fleshy Mango Salsa Salad

In India, the sweet, fleshy, sensual mango is a symbol of love.

Sexy players: tomatoes, sexy spices, citrus, leafy greens

1 ½ cups diced tomatoes

1 cup fresh mango, peeled, seeded and chopped

1 jalapeno pepper, seeded and minced
½ cup red onion, chopped
½ cup cucumber, chopped
2 cloves garlic, chopped
1-2 T freshly squeezed lime juice
lots of fresh cilantro, chopped
1/8 t black pepper
pinch of sea salt
1/2 lb. firm tofu, cut into 1-inch squares, drained of excess water
2 T soy sauce or nama shoyu
1 T toasted sesame oil
3 cups lettuce
olive oil and red wine or apple cider vinegar to taste
pinch of cayenne

(continued on the following page)

Mix soy sauce and sesame oil in a medium - sized bowl. Add the tofu and coat. Refrigerate the tofu, covered, for 1 hour. While the tofu stands, mix all salsa ingredients in a large bowl - (every remaining ingredient except the lettuce, olive oil and vinegar.) Cover and refrigerate. Preheat oven to 350 degrees F and bake the tofu for 30 minutes. Divide the cup of lettuce between 2 plates or large bowls and splash a little oil and vinegar on top. When the tofu is done baking and has cooled, place as much salsa as you like on top of the lettuce and add the tofu. You will have leftover salsa to serve with tortilla chips or whatever you like.

What is love but acceptance of the other, no matter what he is.

- Anais Nin

CHAPTER 4

APPETIZERS A.K.A. FOREPLAY

Hot Fox Sauce (or another salsa to add to your bag o' tricks) ...

Fiery, spontaneous, steady, hot, sometimes naughty, sometimes sweet – this salsa is complex but easy to devour – not unlike your little nymph.

Sexy players: tomatoes, sexy spices

> 1 (16-ounce) can crushed tomatoes, 1 medium-sized yellow onion, peeled & quartered, 2 jalapeno peppers, seeded and sliced, 2 chipotle peppers in adobe sauce (with a bit of their juices from the can), 2 T Worcestershire sauce, 1 T white wine vinegar, 2 t ground cumin, 1 cup fresh cilantro leaves.

Blend all ingredients completely.

It ought to make us feel ashamed when we talk like we know what we're talking about when we talk about love.

- Raymond Carver

Low-Fat Love Potion Hummus

The Chinese used fresh cilantro in love potions and thought it to give immortality. It is after all, one of the oldest herbs on Earth.

Sexy players: sexy spices, almonds, citrus

3 cloves garlic, roughly chopped, 1 jalapeno pepper, seeded and roughly chopped, 1/2 t sea salt, 1/4 t ground chili powder, 1/2 t ground cumin, 1/2 cup cilantro leaves, 1 1/2 cups garbanzo beans, 2 T raw almond butter, juice of 2 lemons, 1/4 cup water.

Pulse garlic, jalapeno, salt, chili powder, cumin and cilantro in a food processor until the garlic is chopped fine. Add garbanzos, almond butter and lemon juice. Process until smooth. Add water and process again for 10 seconds or so, adding more water according to desired consistency. Serve with celery slices, fresh tomatoes, sliced cucumber and homemade pita bread.

What is hell? I maintain that it is the suffering of being unable to love.

- Dostoyevsky

Voluptuous 'Love Apple' Salsa

Choosing spicy chili peppers for your salsa is an art in itself. You may wish to go shopping for fresh chili peppers with your other half, as the mere physicality of its sexy shape can put an open-minded lover in the mood simply by eyeing one.

Sexy players: tomatoes, sexy spices

> **2 cups diced heirloom tomatoes, chopped, 1/2 cup scallions, chopped, 1/3 cup red onion, chopped, 2 cloves garlic, chopped, 1-3 hot peppers of your choice, seeded and minced, juice of 1 lime, 1/2 t cumin, 1/4 t chili powder, pinch of cayenne, pinch of cinnamon, salt and pepper, to taste, 1/2 cup fresh cilantro leaves, chopped, 1/4 cup green olives, chopped.**

> Combine all ingredients in a large bowl and let spices marinade for some time before serving. Enjoy!

I seem to have loved you in numberless forms, numberless times, in life after life, in age after age forever.

-Tagore

Amorous Almond Butter Dip with Raw Veggies

This is a great little snack for the late afternoon or as a precursor to your main meal.

Sexy Players: almonds, citrus, spices

1/4 cup raw almond butter, 1 T pure maple syrup, juice of 1 lemon, 1 T coconut oil, 1 t cayenne pepper, 2 cloves garlic, minced, water, as desired, an assortment of raw veggies.

Chop up your veggies and place them artfully on a serving platter. Blend the remaining ingredients in a blender and pour into a small dipping bowl. A perfect snack to share and feed each other!

Only do not forget, if I wake up crying

it's only because in my dream I'm a lost child

hunting through the leaves of the night for your hands.

- Pablo Neruda

Covetable Carrot Dip with Olives

Both black and green olives are thought to be aphrodisiacs. Some say green for men and black for women.

Sexy players: nutritional yeast, sexy spices

> 1 1/4 cups carrots, steamed and chopped
> 2 T extra-virgin olive oil
> 2 T tahini
> 1 T balsamic vinegar
> 1 T water
> 2 T nutritional yeast
> 1 t garlic, chopped
> 1/2 t red pepper flakes
> a little sea salt and pepper
> 1/4 cup olives of your choice, halved

Place all ingredients (except olives) in a blender or food processor and blend until smooth. Serve with warm pita bread, drizzle with olive oil and garnish with olives.

Your task is not to seek for love, but merely to seek and find all the barriers within yourself that you have built against it.

- Rumi

The Sexual Warrior's Guacamole

Guacamole is the go-to sexy hors d'oeuvre for both men and women. Let these fruity 'testicles' (as the Aztecs called them) work their magic.

Sexy players: avocado, sexy spices, citrus, chia

5 ripe avocados, peeled and seeded, 1 cup chopped red onion, 6 cloves garlic, crushed, 1 jalapeno, seeded and minced, ½ a bunch cilantro leaves, juice of 2 limes, 3 T olive oil, ¼ cup chia gel (basic chia gel = 2 T chia seeds soaked in 1 cup water for 30 min. or longer), sea salt, to taste.

Combine avocado, red onion, garlic, jalapeno and cilantro in a food processor. Add in lime juice, olive oil and sea salt while the food processor is running. Transfer guacamole to your favorite serving bowl and add in the chia gel. Serve with your favorite tortilla chips and raw veggies.

For women, testosterone absorbed from semen can boost her energy.

Wanton Wasabi Avocado Dip

The heat from wasabi peas can rev up your metabolism while their fiber content fills you up – great if you want to shed a few pounds.

Sexy players: avocado, citrus, leafy greens

1 ripe avocado, 2 T, plus 2 t lime juice, 1 cup chopped romaine lettuce, ¼ cup chopped wasabi peas, tortilla chips or raw veggies.

Chop wasabi peas. Cut avocado in half. Delicately remove pit. Scoop avocado into a bowl, preserving the avocado shells and mash. Add lime juice, romaine lettuce and wasabi peas. Mix well and add the spread back into the empty avocado shell. Serve with tortilla chips or veggies.

The Romans divided kissing into three categories:

Osculum for a kiss on the cheek; Basium for a kiss on the lips; Savolium for a deep kiss.

Seductive Sweet Potato Bites

These spicy sweet potato bites are the perfect prelude to the main dish – or the main event!

Sexy players: sexy spices! (coconut oil & sweet potatoes ain't so bad either)

> 4 cups peeled and chopped sweet potatoes
> 1 T coconut oil, melted
> pinch garam masala
> pinch cumin
> dash of cayenne
> pinch of ginger powder
> a bit of sea salt
> a little ground black pepper

Preheat oven to 350 degrees F. On a baking sheet, toss all ingredients. Bake for 35 minutes. Bon appétit!

But hurry, let's entwine ourselves as one, our mouth broken, our soul bitten by love, so time discovers us safely destroyed.

- Federico Garcia Lorca

Argentine Tango Chimichurri Bruschetta

Chimichurri bruschetta is a fitting prelude to a seductive Argentinian tango between two lovers. While tango is the ultimate dance of seduction, chimichurri is the quintessential Argentinian staple.

Sexy players: citrus, sexy spices, avocado

> **Zest of 1 lime, juice of 2 limes, 3 cloves garlic, minced, ¾ t sea salt, ½ t red pepper flakes, ½ a jalapeno, seeded & minced, ¼ t ground black pepper, ¼ cup olive oil, 1 ½ cups cilantro, chopped, 3 avocados, peeled, pitted, cubed, ½ a red onion, chopped, 1 T balsamic vinegar, sliced sourdough bread.**

Combine lime zest, lime juice, vinegar, garlic, salt, red pepper flakes, black pepper, red onion and jalapeno in a bowl. Whisk in the olive oil. Then stir in cilantro. Add in the avocado and stir to combine. Spoon onto toasted sourdough bread and serve.

Kissing at the conclusion of a wedding ceremony can be traced to ancient Roman tradition where a kiss was used to sign a contract.

The Harem's Harissa

Harissa is the ultimate aphrodisiac condiment. Twenty-five red, hot chili peppers?! Baby, watch out!

Sexy players: sexy spices

25 dried hot red chilies
2 T coriander seeds
4 t cumin seeds
2 cloves garlic, minced
6 T virgin olive oil
a touch of sea salt

Soak chilies until they are soft. Toast spices for a few minutes, careful not to burn them and grind them with a mortar and pestle or coffee grinder. Place all ingredients in a blender and combine thoroughly, tasting and adding salt if you wish. Serve with flatbreads, pita chips, as a condiment for lettuce wraps, as a dip for raw veggies....whatever you can think of. This is spicy, so have a cucumber raita or nut milk ready for relief!

Lovers don't finally meet somewhere.
They're in each other all along.

- Rumi

Chapter 5: Sensuous Soups

Pleasure-Seeking Black Bean Soup

This soup is sexy as hell for many reasons. Coconut oil, garlic, onions, carrots, celery, beans, tomatoes, cacao, chili powder and basil – all libido-lovin' goodness!

Sexy players: celery, tomatoes, cacao, sexy spices

1 T virgin coconut oil, 2 cups yellow onions, chopped, 3 cloves garlic, minced, 1 cup carrots, chopped, 1 cup celery, chopped, 5 cans black beans, drained, 1 can diced tomatoes, 5 cups vegetable broth, 4 T raw cacao powder, 1/2 t dried thyme, 1/2 t turmeric, 1/2 t dried rosemary, 2 t cumin, 1 T chili powder, fresh cilantro, as garnish, blue corn tortilla chips, for topping, nutritional yeast, for sprinkling.

In a large stockpot, heat coconut oil over medium heat and cook onions for a few minutes. Add garlic, carrots and celery and cook for another few minutes. Add black beans, tomatoes, vegetable broth cacao and spices. Bring to a boil and let simmer for 30 minutes. Ladle into bowls, garnish with cilantro, tortilla chips and nutritional yeast.

Sensuously-Spiced Sweet Potato Soup

Sweet potatoes are great for your sex life because of their vitamin A content, which helps produce sex hormones while keeping the vagina and uterus in optimal shape.

Sexy players: celery, sexy spices, citrus

2 T coconut oil, 1 small onion, chopped, 2 cloves garlic, minced, 2 stalks celery, chopped, 2 carrots, chopped, 1 jalapeno pepper, seeded and chopped, 2 large sweet potatoes, peeled and cubed, 3 cups vegetable broth, 1 cup water, 1/4 cup raw peanut butter, 1 T ground coriander, 2 t garam masala, 2 T lemon juice, 1/2 t turmeric, 1/2 t ground ginger, 1 t cinnamon, 2 T shoyu or soy sauce, sea salt, to taste, limes wedges to garnish.

In a large pot, sauté onions, garlic, celery, carrots and jalapeno pepper in coconut oil for 5 minutes. Add broth, water and sweet potatoes. Let simmer for 30 minutes. In a small bowl combine peanut butter, lemon juice, spices and soy sauce. Place this mixture in blender. Add soup to blender and blend thoroughly. Season with salt and garnish with lime.

Nothing is mysterious, no human relation. Except love.
                                        -Susan Sontag

Miso Lovely Lentil Soup

This batch makes about 6 servings, depending on your appetite. That said, if you're in for a weekend of lovemaking this will fuel the fires for a while.

Sexy players: celery, tomatoes, spices

> ¼ cup coconut oil
>
> 1 onion chopped
>
> 3 cloves garlic, minced
>
> 2 carrots, peeled and chopped
>
> 2 celery stalks, chopped
>
> 1 russet potato peeled and chopped
>
> 2 T tomato paste
>
> 4 cups water
>
> 2 T red miso
>
> 3 cups water
>
> **(continued on the following page)**

2 cups red lentils

1 t hot sauce (optional)

a touch of sea salt & black pepper

In a large pot, sauté onions and garlic in coconut oil. When translucent and soft add carrots, celery and potatoes. Sauté for five minutes, stirring occasionally. Add tomato paste and 4 cups water.

Continue cooking on medium heat. In another pan, heat 3 cups water over medium heat and add the miso. Mix out the lumps with a spoon or whisk. Add the miso soup and lentils to the large pot. Bring to a boil, then simmer, stirring occasionally. If it is too thick (stew-like) you can add more water. Add hot sauce and adjust seasoning with salt and pepper to taste. Keep on a low simmer for 1 1/2 hours, stirring occasionally. Serve piping hot with freshly ground black pepper, a salad and good bread.

Love is a temporary madness, it erupts like volcanoes and then subsides. And when it subsides, you have to make a decision. You have to work out whether your roots have so entwined together that it is inconceivable that you should ever part. Because this is what love is. Love is not breathlessness. It is not excitement. It is not the promulgation of promises of eternal passion, it is not the desire to mate every second minute of the day, it is not lying awake at night imagining that he is kissing every cranny of your body. No, do not blush. I am telling you some truths. That is just being "in love," which any fool can do. Love itself is what is left over when being in love has burned away, and this is both an art and an unfortunate accident.

- **Louis de Bernieres**

Ravish Me Red Pepper Soup

Red bell peppers are full of vitamins A and C - two vitamins known to support sexual health. Vitamin A has even been known to improve sperm quality.

Sexy players: sexy spices, tomatoes

4 red bell peppers, 1 ½ T coconut oil, 1 ½ cups yellow onion, chopped, 2 cloves garlic, chopped, 1 t cayenne pepper, 1 (14-ounce) can crushed tomatoes, 1 cup coconut milk, 1 cup water, sea salt, to taste, ground pepper, to taste, your favorite hot sauce.

Roast red peppers in an oven at 400 degrees F for approximately 20 minutes. Remove and let cool. Then remove skins and seeds and cut into large pieces. In a large stockpot, heat coconut oil over medium heat. Add onions, garlic and cayenne pepper. Let cook for 5 minutes. Lower heat and add tomatoes, coconut milk, roasted red bell peppers and water. Cook another 10 minutes. Transfer in batches to a blender and blend until smooth. Heat soup over medium heat and serve immediately. Let your lover season his/her own soup with salt, pepper and hot sauce. Serve with good bread and a green salad.

Emotionally, a healthy libido evokes a sense of calm and ease. It fosters intimacy and connection in your relationship.

The Kisser, A Celery-Apple Soup

Like chocolate, apples have that feel-good chemical, phenylethylamine. They're also known to stave off bad breath, keeping your kisser enticing.

Sexy players: celery, sexy spices, citrus

> **2 T coconut oil, 1 cup chopped yellow onion, 2 cloves garlic, minced, 4 cups diced celery, 1 ½ t ground coriander, large pinch sea salt, 3 cups cored and diced apples, 2 cups diced potatoes, 4 cups vegetable broth, juice of 1 lemon.**

Heat coconut oil over medium heat in a large stockpot. Add onion, garlic, celery, coriander and sea salt. Let cook until onions are translucent. Add the remaining ingredients except the lemon juice and bring to a boil. Turn heat to low and let simmer for 20-30 minutes. Let soup cool and then transfer it to a blender in batches. Blend soup well. Add lemon juice before serving.

**The more one judges, the less one loves.
- Honore de Balzac**

Take Me Tomato Coconut Soup

Put the 'love apples' to work in this simple yet sexy tropical soup.

Sexy players: tomatoes, sexy spices, avocado

4 cups organic
tomatoes, chopped
2 t garlic, chopped
1 t pure maple syrup
1 t soy sauce or nama shoyu
1 T lime juice
1 cup coconut milk
¼ t dried ginger
sea salt, to taste
avocado wedges, for topping

Blend all ingredients (except avocado wedges) until smooth and creamy. Top with avocado wedges. Share with your inamorato/a.

A one-minute kiss can burn 26 calories.

Bewitching Sumac Soup

Sumac, an obscure berry growing on bushes throughout the Mediterranean - mainly in southern Italy and throughout the Middle East, is a mysterious and exotic little thing that's best eaten slowly and sensuously.

Sexy players: whole grains, sexy spices

1 cup brown basmati rice, ½ cup green lentils, 1 ½ T sumac, 2 cups fresh parsley, minced, 2 cups fresh cilantro, minced, 1 cup chopped onion, 3 cloves garlic, minced, ½ t turmeric, 1 T extra-virgin olive oil, sea salt & black pepper, to taste.

Cover rice and lentils with water. Bring to a boil and simmer for 40 minutes. Add parsley, cilantro and sumac to the pot. In a pan, sauté onions, garlic and turmeric in olive oil over low-heat for ten minutes. Add to soup. Season with salt and pepper. Serve hot in two bowls with fresh bread.

Orgasms are believed to fight infection, increasing the body's infection-busting cells by twenty percent!

Sexy & Slow-Cooked Tomato Soup with Chickpeas, Brown Rice, Roasted Garlic and Spices

With an entire head of garlic and a multitude of aphrodisical spices, this slow-cooked bowl of love will cure what ails you.

Sexy players: whole grains, tomatoes, sexy spices

> **1/3 cup garbanzo beans, ¼ cup brown rice, 3 cups water, 2 cinnamon sticks, 1 (14-ounce) can diced tomatoes, 1 t garam masala, ½ t curry powder, ½ t cumin seeds, ½ t fennel seeds, ½ t turmeric, 4 whole cloves, 1/8 t chili powder, pinch cayenne pepper, ½ jalapeno pepper, seeded and minced, 1 head garlic, roasted, 1/8 t ground black pepper, pinch sea salt, 2 T cilantro leaves.**

Roast your garlic. Place all ingredients except cilantro & including roasted & peeled garlic in a slow-cooker. Cook on low for 5-6 hours. Remove cinnamon sticks and cloves, ladle into two bowls and garnish with cilantro. Serve with a warm baguette.

Bedroom Bliss

Your bedroom is the most intimate room in your home, a place where you can relax, indulge your senses and let go of the day. It's a place to dream, heal, hide, whisper and make love. Choose bedding, linens and blankets that are not only beautiful, but which resonate on a deeper level. As with food choices, making informed purchases by choosing organic and socially responsible products for your bedroom gives you a sense of connection with the natural world while giving back to the greater good. Select alternatives to synthetics - like cotton, wool, down, and silk. Put a canopy over your bed – perhaps a soft white mosquito net or a silk shawl – to create the illusion of being in your own little seductive world.

When you truly find love, you find yourself. Therefore, the path to love is our spiritual destiny.

- Deepak Chopra

The Damsel's 13-Bean Soup

This sexy stew will alleviate all distress upon first bite.

Sexy players: the whole damn thing

1 ½ cups Bob's Red Mill 13-bean soup mix, soaked in water, overnight.

2 T coconut oil

7-10 cloves garlic, peeled

2 cups yellow onion, chopped

2 carrots, peeled and chopped

1 cup chopped celery

1 T fresh ginger root, chopped

pinch cayenne

dash of cumin

a bit of turmeric

pinch garam masala

4 cups vegetable broth

1 cup water

(continued on following page)

1 (14-ounce) can diced tomatoes

1 t soy sauce or nama shoyu

juice of half a lemon

sea salt, to taste

ground black pepper, to taste

handful fresh parsley

nutritional yeast, to taste

In a large stockpot, heat coconut oil over medium heat. Sauté garlic, onion, carrots, celery and ginger for 5 minutes. Add spices. Cook another 5 minutes. Add broth, tomatoes, drained beans, water, soy sauce and lemon juice. Bring to a boil. Let simmer, partially covered for about an hour. Add salt and pepper. Serve and garnish with parsley. Sprinkle with nutritional yeast. Bon appétit!

There are only three things to be done with a woman. You can love her, suffer for her, or turn her into literature.

- Henry Miller

Tenderly Slow-Cooked Lentil Soup with Chipotle Peppers

A cozy little soup with a treasure trove of nutrient-rich foods for your sex drive.

Sexy players: tomatoes, sexy spices, leafy greens

1 lb. red lentils, 1 yellow onion, chopped, 2 carrots, chopped, 3 cloves garlic, minced, 1 (14 – ounce) can diced tomatoes, ½ t oregano, 2 canned chipotle peppers, in adobe sauce, sea salt, to taste, black pepper, to taste, water, 4 cups arugula.

Wash lentils well and place all ingredients except arugula in a slow-cooker. Cover with water. Cook over medium-heat for four hours. Adjust seasonings and stir in arugula before serving. Enjoy with a warm baguette and fresh salad.

Only the united beat of sex and heart together can create ecstasy.

- Anais Nin

Chapter 6: Gratifying Grains

Passionate Porridge

Think you might be kept inside for a long weekend of lovemaking because it's snowing outside and you can't bear the thought of leaving your cozy little apartment? If so, double the dose on this one.

Sexy players: oats, dates, chia, almonds

> **1 cup oat groats, 6 cups water, 2 cinnamon sticks, ¼ t sea salt, 4 Medjool dates, pitted and chopped, 4 dried figs, chopped, 1 T chia seeds, soaked overnight, unsweetened almond milk, to taste, ground cinnamon, to taste.**

Place oat groats, water, cinnamon sticks and sea salt in a slow-cooker and cook on a low setting, overnight. In the morning when you are ready to eat, add the dates, figs and chia gel. Serve in 2 bowls, pouring almond milk in, to taste. Sprinkle with ground cinnamon.

> **Love is a smoke made with the fume of sighs.**
>
> **-William Shakespeare**

Forbidden Blueberry Black Rice Pudding

There's simply something sexy about eating a dish with the word "forbidden." Forbidden black rice transforms from black to purple when cooked, and with the addition of blueberries, you'll have a marvelous feast for the eyes on your breakfast table. If you're lacking a breakfast table, take it to the bedroom. Set empty dishes aside and get busy.

Sexy players: whole grains, almonds, sexy spices, vanilla

½ cup forbidden black rice, 4-5 cups water, pinch sea salt, 2 cups almond milk, 2 cinnamon sticks, 2 T raw honey, 1 t pure vanilla extract, 2 cups blueberries.

Cook rice in the water over medium heat for one hour. Add remaining ingredients, stir and simmer for another 15 minutes. Remove cinnamon sticks and serve.

When I'm good, I'm very good, but when I'm bad, I'm better.

- Mae West

A Coquette's Strawberry Oatmeal

When the weather turns cold and all you want to do is stay in bed and cuddle with your honey, lure him or her out of bed with the aroma of oatmeal baking in the oven.

Sexy players: oats, almonds, sexy spices, vanilla, strawberries

2 T coconut oil, 1 cup rolled oats, ¼ cup chopped almonds, 1 T flaxseeds, 2 T raw agave nectar, ½ t baking powder, 1 t ground cinnamon, 1 cup almond milk, 1 flax egg (1 T flaxseed, whisked with 3 T warm water), 1 t pure vanilla extract, ½ cup coconut flakes, 1 cup strawberries, sliced.

Preheat oven to 350 degrees F. Combine all ingredients in a large bowl. Lightly coat a baking dish with coconut oil. Transfer mix to baking dish and bake for 30 minutes. Serve warm.

Love is like a fever which comes and goes quite independently of the will...there are no age limits for love.

- Stendhal

Beautiful Biriyani

Brown rice provides our bodies with magnesium, which aids in muscle contraction - the physical mechanics of orgasm.

Sexy players: whole grains, sexy spices, almonds

1 T coconut oil
1 onion, chopped
2 cloves garlic, minced
2 carrots, grated
1/2 cup long-grain brown rice, soaked overnight
1 t cumin seeds
1 t ground coriander
1 t yellow mustard seeds
1 t ground cardamom
2 cups vegetable stock
1 bay leaf
salt and pepper, to taste
1/4 cup chopped almonds
fresh parsley or cilantro, as garnish

(continued on the following page)

Heat the coconut oil over medium-low heat in a large pot and cook the onion for 3-5 minutes. Add garlic and carrots and cook for another 3-5 minutes. Drain the rice and add it with the spices to the pot. Cook for another 1-2 minutes, stirring to coat the grains in oil and spices. Pour in the stock, add the bay leaf and season with salt and pepper. Bring to a boil. Cover and simmer for 30 minutes or more, adding more water if need be. Remove from heat and let sit for 5 minutes. Discard bay leaf. Stir in the nuts and garnish with cilantro or parsley.

What I cannot love, I overlook.

-Anais Nin

Irresistible Indonesian Brown Rice

The allicin in garlic is thought to get the blood flowing to your sex organs while the chili peppers in this dish will release natural endorphins known to get you high and feeling blissful.

Sexy players: whole grains, sexy spices, citrus

1 cup brown basmati rice, 2 ½ cups water, 2 T coconut oil, 1 cup yellow onions, chopped, 8 cloves garlic, chopped, 2 T ginger root, chopped, 14 Thai red chilies, 4 T dried coconut shreds, juice of 2 limes, 1 ½ cups coconut milk, sea salt, to taste, ground black pepper, to taste, lime wedges, for garnish, mint sprigs for garnish, green onions, for garnish.

Cover rice with water and cook as you normally would. In a saucepan, heat oil on medium heat, add onions and cook for 3 minutes, followed by the garlic, ginger and chilies. Cook another 3-5 minutes. Turn heat off. When the rice is finished, pour it into the saucepan and coat with oil and spices. Add coconut, lime juice & coconut milk. Combine well. Add salt & pepper. Serve in two bowls. Garnish with lime wedges, green onions & sprigs of mint.
Only in love are unity and duality not in conflict.

- Tagore

Captivating Couscous with Red Peppers and Harem's Harissa

Slip away on a magic carpet ride with an exotic bowl of couscous.

Sexy players: whole grains, sexy spices, citrus

1 cup couscous, water, pinch sea salt, 2 t olive oil, 1/4 cup parsley, minced, 2 cloves garlic, minced, 1 roasted red bell pepper, peeled, seeded and sliced thin, Harem's Harissa, on the side (see p. 79), lemon wedges, as garnish.

Place couscous in a medium-sized stockpot. Cover with water and bring to a boil. Lower heat to a simmer and let cook for 7 minutes or so. Drain water if there's any remaining. Add in olive oil and toss. Add remaining ingredients except harissa and lemon wedges and toss. When you are ready to serve, do so with lemon wedges and Harem's Harissa.

Love doesn't need reason. It speaks from the irrational wisdom of the heart.

- Deepak Chopra

Waxing Wheat Berry Salad

Wheat berries are rich with fiber, protein and vitamin E (our delicious little sex nutrient).

Sexy players: whole grains, leafy greens, citrus, sexy spices

> **1/2 cup wheat berries**
>
> **2 T dried cranberries or raisins**
>
> **3 T raw pine nuts**
>
> **2 T chopped red onion**
>
> **1 cup shredded romaine lettuce**
>
> **1 T flaxseeds**
>
> **1 T lemon juice**
>
> **1 T olive oil**
>
> **1 T soy sauce or shoyu**
>
> **pinch cayenne pepper**
>
> **pinch ground black pepper**
>
> **pinch sea salt**
>
> **handful of your favorite herbs**

Cook wheat berries as you would pasta. Drain and place in a large bowl. Add remaining ingredients and mix well. Enjoy!

Bella Basil's Basmati Rice Salad

Did you know that the ancient Greeks fed basil to their horses before breeding time? Just the aroma of fresh basil is a major turn on.

Sexy players: whole grains, celery, almonds, citrus

1 cup brown basmati rice, 3/4 cup chopped yellow onions, 4-5 cloves garlic, minced, 1/4 cup carrots, chopped, 1 celery stalk, diced, 1 T extra-virgin coconut oil, 1/4 cup raw almonds, chopped or sliced thin, 1/8 cup raw sunflower seeds, 3 T soy sauce or shoyu, 1 T rice vinegar, 1 T pure maple syrup, 1 T lime juice, a few handfuls of lettuce greens, 2 handfuls fresh basil.

Cook rice as you normally would. While rice is cooking, heat coconut oil in a large pan. Add onions, garlic, carrots and celery. Cook over medium low heat for 7-10 minutes. While veggies are cooking, combine dressing ingredients in a small bowl - (soy sauce, vinegar, maple syrup and lime juice). Add almonds and sunflower seeds to the veggies and cook for another 3 minutes. Toss all players, including lettuce and basil in a serving bowl. Enjoy!

Chastity's Cucumber Brown Rice Sweet Potato Salad

Every ingredient in this salad has some version or other of libido lovin' goodness. This salad is great for breakfast, lunch or dinner.

Sexy players: whole grains, sea veggies, sexy spices

> 1/4 cup brown rice
> 1 1/2 cups sweet potato, peeled and chopped into small cubes
> 3/4 cup cucumber, peeled and chopped into small cubes
> 1/4 cup chopped sweet onion
> 1/2 a nori sheet, torn into small pieces and soaked
> 1 T sesame seeds (toasted)

> For the dressing:

> 1 T mellow white miso
> 1 T chopped fresh ginger
> 1 T water
> 2 T grapeseed oil
> 1 T rice vinegar
> 1 t soy sauce or nama shoyu
> 1-2 T ground flaxseeds

(continued on the following page)

1 t raw sugar (optional)
2 t seaweed gomasio (optional)
pinch crushed red pepper flakes

Cook rice and boil sweet potatoes as you normally would. While the rice and potatoes are cooking, soak the nori and toast the sesame seeds. Watch them carefully as they tend to burn easily. Whisk all dressing ingredients together in a medium bowl. When rice and sweet potatoes are finished cooking, drain them and add to a large serving bowl. Add the cucumbers, nori and onions. Pour in the dressing and toss to make sure the salad is evenly coated. Top with toasted sesame seeds and serve immediately.

Quinoa, Nature's Sexiest Grain

Quinoa gets its very own section because it is one of the healthiest whole grains on the planet. It's also one of the most charming of the whole grain players because it's a complete protein with nine amino acids required of us to thrive in the sac. One serving of quinoa (about ¼ cup) gives us 48% of our daily magnesium needs. Quinoa has zero cholesterol and a mere 13 mg of sodium per serving, (two of our villains when eaten in excess). Quinoa is a South American native and can be red, white or black. It can also be cooked in a mere ten minutes – great for the modern day lover!

Sweet Aztec Porridge

Quinoa once played a ceremonial role in ancient Aztec and Mayan cultures. How might you present this dish in a ritualistic way? Sex and food are much sweeter when we give them the mindful reverence they deserve. This dish is perfect for a sacred beginning to a lover's day.

Sexy players: whole grains, almonds, banana, maca, sexy spices

1 cup cooked quinoa, ½ cup almond milk, 1 banana, 1 t maca powder, ½ t nutmeg, ½ t cinnamon, 2 t raw honey, pinch sea salt.

Place all ingredients in your blender and blend until creamy. Serve in two bowls and sprinkle with cinnamon.

It was love at first sight, at last sight, at ever and ever sight.

- Vladimir Nabokov

Kissable Coconut-Cauliflower-Swiss Chard-Quinoa

Cauliflower is full of vitamin C, which is necessary for the synthesis of hormones that turn us on.

Sexy players: leafy greens, whole grains, sexy spices

2 cups chopped cauliflower, 7-10 Swiss chard leaves, rinsed & chopped, 1/3 cup quinoa, 2 cloves garlic, minced, 1 cup yellow onions, chopped, 2 T extra-virgin coconut oil, 1 t turmeric, 1/2 t cinnamon, 1/2 t coriander, 1 t cumin, chili powder, to taste, sea salt and black pepper, to taste, 2 T pure maple syrup, 2/3 cup coconut milk.

Cook quinoa as you normally would. Steam cauliflower and Swiss chard. In a large sauté pan, heat coconut oil over medium heat and cook onions and garlic for five minutes. Add remaining ingredients, including the quinoa, cauliflower and Swiss chard. Combine well. Let simmer for 10 minutes and serve in two bowls.

Love is the beginning of the journey, its end, and the journey itself.

-Deepak Chopra

Kiss Me Kitchari

Kitchari was born from the science of Ayurveda, India's ancient healing tradition. Said to support the digestive system and rid the body of toxins, kitchari is a super sexy dish for the autumn and winter months.

Sexy players: whole grains, leafy greens, sexy spices, citrus

2 cups vegetable broth

2 cups water

¾ cup quinoa

¾ cup red lentils

6 cloves garlic, minced

1 cup yellow onion, chopped

½ cup carrots, chopped

1 cup frozen spinach

1 cup frozen broccoli

½ t turmeric

¼ t cayenne pepper

¼ t ground ginger

2 t soy sauce or nama shoyu

(continued on the following page)

1 T lime juice

2 t toasted sesame oil

sea salt, black pepper, to taste

½ cup fresh cilantro, minced

In a medium-sized stockpot, add water, broth, quinoa and lentils. Bring to a boil and immediately turn heat down to a simmer. Add in garlic, onions and carrots. Cook for 15 minutes. Add in spinach and broccoli. Cook for another 10 minutes. Add remaining ingredients, cook for another 5 minutes, adding more liquid if necessary. Serve warm.

A thousand half-loves must be forsaken to take one whole heart home.

- Rumi

Yoga is a great tool to enhance the quality of our sex lives. One great asana is seated butterfly pose. This posture improves blood flow to the pelvic area and helps increase sensation.

Love Me Lemon-Spinach Quinoa

Co-enzyme q-10 is a little enzyme found in raw spinach that is known to increase sperm count in men. Looking to make a baby? Eat your greens. Baby-making or not – still eat your greens!

Sexy players: whole grains, citrus, leafy greens, sexy spices, almonds

½ **cup quinoa, 1 clove garlic, pressed, zest of 1 lemon, juice of 1 lemon, 1-2 t balsamic vinegar, sea salt, to taste, black pepper, to taste, pinch of crushed red pepper flakes, 1 ½ T extra-virgin olive oil, 1/4 cup red onion, diced, 1/3 cup black olives, diced, 4 cups tightly packed spinach leaves, handful fresh basil, torn into small pieces, handful slivered almonds.**

In a stockpot, combine quinoa and 1 cup water. Bring to a boil and let simmer for several minutes, until quinoa is cooked through. In a large bowl combine garlic, lemon zest, lemon juice, vinegar, spices and olive oil. Add quinoa and remaining ingredients to dressing. Toss to combine.

Reason is powerless in the expression of love.

- Rumi

Libido-Lovin' Quinoa Salad

You can't go wrong with this baby. Every ingredient here will give your sex life a loving boost.

Sexy Players: whole grains, chia, almonds, avocado, sexy spices

1 cup quinoa, 2 cups water, 1 T chia seeds, 1 T chopped or slivered almonds, 2 T dried cranberries, 1 T chopped pecans, 2 T chopped red onions, ½ of an apple, diced, 1 ripe avocado, peeled, seeded & chopped.

Dressing:

1 clove garlic, minced, 2 T olive oil, juice of ½ a lemon, pinch of chili powder.

Place quinoa in water and bring to a boil. Let simmer for ten minutes. Transfer cooked quinoa to a large serving bowl. Add in the remaining ingredients and toss with the dressing. Season with sea salt and ground black pepper.

Have a stuffy nose? Have sex! It's a natural antihistamine.

Erotic Quinoa Tabouleh

A quinoa tabouleh is simply sexier for your organs than its traditional bulgur counterpart.

Sexy players: whole grains, citrus, sexy spices

> **1 cup quinoa**
> **2 cups water**
> **1 grapefruit, peeled and segmented**
> **1/2 cup raisins**
> **1/4 cup fresh basil, torn**
> **1/2 cup pistachios, shelled**
> **1 T lemon juice**
> **1 T extra-virgin olive oil**
> **1 clove garlic, pressed**
> **pinch of cayenne**
> **pinch sea salt**

Bring quinoa to a boil in the water, let simmer for 10 minutes. Let cool. Place quinoa, grapefruit, raisins, pistachios and basil in a large bowl. In a smaller bowl, mix lemon juice, olive oil, garlic, cayenne and salt together. Combine dressing with salad and toss.

Men who kiss their wives in the morning live 5 years longer than those who don't.

Venus' Fertility Quinoa Salad

Arugula was born in the Mediterranean, one of the most fertile and romantic strips of land on Earth. It is considered to support male and female sex drive, increase fertility and alleviate anxiety in the bedroom.

Sexy players: whole grains, avocado, leafy greens, tomatoes, citrus

> 1/2 cup quinoa
>
> 4 cups arugula
>
> 1 ripe avocado, peeled, seeded and sliced
>
> 1 medium tomato, chopped
>
> 1-2 cloves garlic, minced
>
> 2 T lemon juice
>
> a little sea salt and pepper

Cook quinoa as you normally would. (I usually use a little more than twice as much water than quinoa and cook for 10-15 minutes). Place arugula, avocado, tomato, garlic and 1 T of the lemon juice in a large bowl. Add in the cooked quinoa and remaining lemon juice. Season with salt and pepper. Toss to combine.

Chapter 7: Divine Desserts

Luscious Lemon Cake

While sugar is not the best for our sexy vegan diet, citrus and a little indulgence from time to time certainly is!

Sexy players: whole grains, vanilla, citrus

½ cup quinoa flour, ½ cup whole-wheat pastry flour, ½ cup all-purpose flour, ½ cup coconut sugar, 1 t baking soda, 4 T coconut oil, melted, 1 t apple cider vinegar, 1 t pure vanilla extract, juice of 1 large lemon, 2 T lemon zest, ½ cup water.

Preheat oven to 350 degrees F. Lightly oil a small loaf pan, approximately 3x7 inches in size. Combine flours, sugar, baking soda and lemon zest. In another bowl, combine coconut oil, vinegar, vanilla, lemon juice and water. Add wet ingredients to dry ones and mix well. Spoon into loaf pan and bake for 25-30 minutes. Serve warm with a smear of coconut oil.

We love because it's the only true adventure.

- Nikki Giovanni

Beatific Banana Spelt Bread

This divine treat may also be served for breakfast if you wish.

> **Sexy players:** bananas, vanilla, whole grains, almonds

2 ripe bananas, mashed, ½ t pure vanilla extract, 1/8 cup pure maple syrup, 1/8 cup sunflower oil, ¾ cup spelt flour, 1/8 cup almond meal, 1 T flaxseed, ½ t baking soda, ½ t baking powder, dash of sea salt, dash of cinnamon.

Preheat oven to 350 degrees F. Lightly oil a loaf baking dish, approx. 3 X 7 inches in size. In one bowl, mix mashed bananas, vanilla, maple syrup and sunflower oil. In another bowl, combine spelt flour, almond meal, flaxseed, baking soda, baking powder, sea salt and cinnamon. Combine wet ingredients with the dry ones and pour into the baking dish. Bake for 25 minutes or so.

From a little spark may burst a flame.

- Dante Alighieri

Sinful Strawberry Shortcake

Who isn't aroused by the languid scent of a slightly sweet aroma wafting from a warm oven? Bake your mate this exotic take on a traditional favorite.

Sexy players: whole grains, almonds, vanilla, strawberries

1 cup quinoa flour

1 cup whole-wheat pastry flour

¼ cup flaxseeds

¾ cup coconut sugar, plus a pinch for topping

1 t baking powder

½ t baking soda

¼ t sea salt

2/3 cup almond milk

¼ cup coconut oil, melted

1 T pure vanilla extract

handful sliced strawberries, for topping

splash of almond milk

(continued on the following page)

Preheat oven to 350 degrees F. With a little coconut oil, lightly oil a mini loaf pan approx. 3 X 7 inches in size. Mix all dry ingredients in a large bowl. Combine all wet ingredients in a small bowl. Add wet ingredients to dry ones (leaving strawberries out of the mix) and combine well. Transfer dough to your baking dish, sprinkle top with a bit more sugar and bake for 25 minutes. Serve in bowls. Top with strawberries and a splash of almond milk.

A kiss transmits smells, tastes, sound and tactile signals that all affect how individuals perceive each other and ultimately, whether they will kiss again.

Delicate Date Muffins

Just one tablespoon of flaxseed a day helps increase testosterone, the chemical with the greatest effect on libido. Both walnuts and flaxseeds contain essential fatty acids - the building blocks of sex hormones.

Sexy players: oats & whole grains, sexy spices, dates, almonds

1 cup spelt flour, 1/2 cup whole wheat flour, 3/4 cup flaxseeds, 3/4 cup rolled oats, 2 t baking soda, 1/2 t sea salt, 2 t cinnamon, 1 cup dates, chopped, 1 cup walnuts, chopped, 3/4 cup almond milk, 2 flax eggs (2 T flaxseed mixed with 6 T water), 1/2 cup raw honey, 1/4-1/2 cup water.

Preheat oven to 350 degrees F. In a small bowl, combine almond milk, flax eggs, honey and water. In a larger bowl combine remaining ingredients. Add wet ingredients to dry ingredients and mix well, adding more water if need be. Add batter to a lined or oiled muffin tin and bake for 20 minutes. Yields: Approx. 16 muffins. Enjoy!

i like my body when it is with your

body. It is so quite a new thing.

Muscles better and nerves more.

i like your body, I like what it does,

i like its hows, I like to feel the
spine

of your body and its bones, and the
trembling

-firm-smoothness and which i will

again and again and again

kiss, i like kissing this and that of
you,

i like, slowly stroking the, shocking
fuzz

of your electric furr, and what-is-it
comes

over parting flesh ..... and eyes big
love-crumbs,

and possibly I like the thrill

of under me you so quite new.

                              - E. E.
                              Cummings

Virtuous Lemon-Thyme Mini Muffins

Ancient Romans were known to combine thyme with roses to prepare their houses for orgies …

Sexy players: whole grains, citrus, vanilla

1/4 cup, plus 2 T spelt flour
1/4 t sea salt
1/2 t baking powder
2 T flaxseed
6 T water
1/8 cup grapeseed oil
1/8 cup agave nectar
1 1/2 t dried thyme
1 T fresh lemon zest
½ t pure vanilla extract

Preheat oven to 350 degrees F. In a medium-sized bowl, combine flour, baking powder and sea salt. In a small bowl, mix flaxseed and water together. Add the flax paste to the dry ingredients. Slowly add in the oil, agave nectar, thyme, lemon zest and vanilla. Scoop batter into an oiled mini muffin pan. Bake for 20 minutes. Let cool and serve with a smear of coconut oil.

Oh, So Sexy Oatmeal Cookies

Who doesn't love oatmeal cookies freshly baked, and oozing with comfort? Your sweetie will love this version, especially in the autumn when the leaves turn and the air emanates its chill, beckoning baked oatmeal cookies and extended bouts of skin-to-skin.

Sexy players: oats & other whole grains, sexy spices

1 cup rolled oats, 1 cup whole wheat pastry flour, 2 T flaxseeds, 1 t baking powder, 1 t baking soda, 2 t cinnamon, pinch sea salt, ¼ cup coconut sugar, ¼ cup coconut oil, melted, 2/3 cup pumpkin puree.

Preheat oven to 350 degrees F. Lightly oil a baking sheet with coconut oil. In a large bowl, combine all ingredients except coconut oil and pumpkin puree. In a smaller bowl, whisk coconut oil and pumpkin puree together. Add them to the mix and combine batter completely. Form cookie batter into round balls (size is up to you) and flatten them with your hand. Bake for 10-15 minutes, depending on size and oven.

Love is the extremely difficult realization that someone other than oneself is real.

- Iris Murdoch

Avocado Cacao Cake of Adonis

Deeply delightful and decadent, this one takes the cake for special occasions. If you're feeling festive, gather the following love-inducing ingredients and put your baking cap on!

Sexy players: whole grains, cacao, vanilla, avocado

2 cups spelt flour, 1 cup gluten-free, all-purpose flour, 2 t baking powder, 2 t baking soda, 6 T raw cacao powder, 1 cup raw sugar, pinch sea salt, 2 t pure vanilla extract, dash of cinnamon, 1 ripe avocado, mashed, ¼ cup coconut oil, melted, 2 cups water, 1 T raw apple cider vinegar.

Preheat oven to 350 degrees F and oil up two circular baking dishes approx. 8 inches in size. In a large bowl, combine all dry ingredients, except the sugar. In another bowl, combine wet ingredients, including the mashed avocado. Combine both bowls, incorporating sugar and mix well. Divide batter equally among both dishes and bake for 30 minutes. Let cool and frost one round with your favorite frosting. Place the second round on top and frost that one. Enjoy!

Love yourself first and everything falls into line. You really have to love yourself to get anything done in this world.

- Lucille Ball

Adorable Almond Butter Cookies

The first time I made these cookies, I ate half the batch in one day. They are delicate and melt in your mouth – like the best kisses do. Enjoy these libido-boosting delicacies – and don't forget to share!

Sexy players: almonds, dates

1 cup raw almond butter

12 Medjool dates, pitted

1 T coconut oil

1 t pure vanilla extract

¼ t sea salt

Preheat oven to 350 degrees F. In a food processor, combine all ingredients until they form a dough-like mixture. Scoop tablespoon-sized rounds onto an oiled or lined cookie sheet. Flatten the rounds a little with a fork. Bake for about 10 minutes. Remove these delicate morsels with care and let cool.

Pan's Potent Acai Power Bowl

Surprise your sweetie with this sexy superfood dessert and you may find yourself strapped beneath the sheets!

Sexy players: acai, strawberries, maca, chia, vanilla, banana

1 (3 ½ ounce) package Sambazon frozen Acai

1 cup frozen, organic strawberries

1 t maca powder

1 t chia seeds

1 T raw honey

¼ cup granola

¼ cup almond milk

¼ t pure vanilla extract

¼ cup banana chips

Place all ingredients in a blender and blend until smooth.

Love is the cheapest of religions.

- Cesare Pavese

Ambrosial Mango Carpaccio

Spice up a sexy little mango with a touch of cayenne and you're in for a real treat.

Sexy players: citrus, sexy spices

> **1 ripe mango, seeded & sliced**
>
> **juice of ½ a lemon**
>
> **1 T agave nectar**
>
> **½ t cayenne pepper**

Place mango on a large plate. In a small bowl, mix the remaining ingredients. Drizzle over mango slices and place in the fridge for a half hour or so. Enjoy together.

You don't find love, it finds you. It's got a little bit to do with destiny, with fate, and what's written in the stars.

- Anais Nin

Crazy-For-You Cacao Popsicles

Play, play, play. That's the name of the game for these slippery treats. Escape back to your days of youth. Be a kid again. And love like you always knew how to love.

Sexy players: cacao

¼ **cup raw cacao powder**

1 **cup coconut milk**

2 **T agave nectar**

Blend all ingredients in a blender and pour into popsicle molds. Freeze for 5 hours or more. Enjoy while walking, skipping and jumping - hand-in-hand.

For many men, simply watching a woman eat arouses thoughts of oral sex. Cacao popsicles should do the trick.

Seraphic Strawberries & Kitty's Almond Kreme

You simply can't go wrong with this treat – especially during the warmer months.

Sexy players: strawberries, almonds, vanilla, dates

> **1 cup raw almonds**
>
> **½ t pure vanilla extract**
>
> **2 Medjool dates, seeded and soaked in ½ cup water**
>
> **1 ½ cups water**
>
> **2 cups organic strawberries, sliced**
>
> **raw agave or honey, for drizzling**

Soak raw almonds in purified water for 24 hours. Drain. Remove peels and place them in a blender. Add the water, vanilla and dates. Blend until thick. Divide strawberries among two bowls and dollop the kitty kreme on top. Drizzle with agave or honey.

Female orgasms can actually cure headaches due to the release of endorphins.

Soothing Strawberry Soft Serve

This terribly healthy dessert is so simple if you have a food processor or high-speed blender. Sugar is a bad form of energy because it hits the bloodstream quickly, spiking blood sugar levels. Then, you experience a sudden crash, leaving the body exhausted for sustained sexual adventures. The touch of maple syrup here will satisfy your sweet tooth while fortifying your body with 20 health-promoting compounds.

Sexy players: strawberries, sexy spices

3 T coconut oil, melted
1 T pure maple syrup
dash of cinnamon
1 (16-ounce) bag frozen strawberries, (preferably organic)

Place frozen strawberries in a food processor and let sit for 20 minutes. In a small bowl, mix coconut oil, maple syrup and cinnamon together until well combined. Add coconut oil mixture to food processor and pulse everything until smooth. Serve in two delicate bowls and drizzle a little maple syrup on top.

The supreme happiness of life is the conviction that we are loved.
- Victor Hugo

Chia Warrior Pudding

One of the most popular ways to eat the sexual warrior chia seeds, chia puddings are easy to make and fun for everyone.

Sexy players: almonds, chia, dates, vanilla

1 cup almond milk

¼ cup chia seeds

1 T rose water

¼ cup date crumbles

2 T shredded coconut

½ t pure vanilla extract

a dash of cinnamon

Place all ingredients in a large bowl. Stir to combine. Let sit for 30 minutes. Serve in 2 bowls. Bon appétit!

I love you as certain dark things are to be loved, in secret, between the shadow and the soul.

- Pablo Neruda

Chillout Chia-Berry Popsicles

When the summer months set in and you need a bite to cool you off after a steamy sexcapade, let these babies invigorate and rejuvenate.

Sexy players: chia

1/3 cup chia gel (basic chia gel = 4 T chia seeds soaked in 2 cups water for 30 min. or longer. Make an ample amount and store in the fridge to have on hand for an immediate energy-libido boost.)

1/3 cup frozen, organic blueberries

pure maple syrup or raw honey, to taste

Blend blueberries and sweetener of your choice in a high-speed blender. Add chia gel. Blend further. Pour mixture into popsicle molds and place in freezer. Let freeze for at least five hours. Eat as desired.

Sex is one of the nine reasons for reincarnation. The other eight are unimportant.

- Henry Miller

The Lovesick Avocado-Chocolate Mousse

This is one of those perfectly erotic, creamy foods that should truly be taken in some creative way. From each other's flesh, perhaps?

Sexy players: avocados, cacao, vanilla, sexy spices

   2 ripe avocados, pitted and peeled

   ¼ cup raw cacao powder

   ¼ cup pure maple syrup

   ¼ cup water

   1 T pure vanilla extract

   ¼ t sea salt

   ¼ t cayenne pepper

Blend. Serve to 2 hungry and soulful lovers.

For one human being to love another: that is perhaps the most difficult of all our tasks, the ultimate, the last test and proof, the work for which all other work is but preparation.

                        - Mae West

Aphrodite's Acai Sorbet

A light sorbet serves as the perfect exclamation point to any dinner. It will certainly not weigh you down when it's time to move to the boudoir.

Sexy players: acai, citrus

> **2 packets Sambazon frozen acai**
>
> **2 T unrefined extra-virgin coconut oil**
>
> **2 T raw honey**
>
> **lemon or lime slices**

Let acai unthaw a bit. Melt coconut oil. Place all ingredients in a high-speed blender and blend until smooth. Serve in 2 glass bowls with a slice of lemon or lime.

There are two ways to reach me: by way of kisses or by way of the imagination. But there is a hierarchy: the kisses alone don't work.

- Anais Nin

Sweetly Raw Banana Pudding with Rose Water

Rose water, like chocolate, contains phenylethylamine, (that chemical that produces the feeling of post-coital bliss). What's more, it's great to use on your body - (think refreshing rosewater facial splash).

Sexy players: bananas, sexy spices

½ **cup raw cashews, soaked**

2 large bananas

ground cardamom, to taste

splash of rose water

Drain the cashews of water and blend the cashews and banana together. Spoon into two dishes and splash a little rosewater on each, then sprinkle with cardamom.

Potassium is a key nutrient for muscle strength, including your pelvic muscles. Think kegel exercises and bananas for more intense contractions when you orgasm.

Unrequited Chocolate-Chia-Oat Pudding

Cacao, chia & oats take center stage in this rich and creamy pudding, sure to boost any lagging libido and/or scorned lover.

Sexy players: chia, oats, cacao, vanilla, sexy spices

1 ½ cups coconut milk

2 T chia seeds

¼ cup rolled oats

3 T cacao powder

2-3 T pure maple syrup

½ t pure vanilla extract

dash of cinnamon

In a large bowl, whisk all ingredients together until cacao powder is totally absorbed. Let sit for 30 minutes in the fridge or at room temperature – up to you. Scoop the rich, creamy pudding into two small bowls and eat slowly – with mindfulness and pleasure.

Art, even the angriest and darkest, is created out of love.

- Meredith Monk

Beso's Blueberry-Avocado-Maca Pudding

The maca plant lives in the high altitudes of the mountains of Peru at 7,000 to 11,000 feet, making it the highest growing plant on Earth. It provides a myriad of health benefits to the body – sexual stimulation, fertility support, treatment of sexual dysfunction, glandular support and hormonal balance.

Sexy players: avocado, chia, dates, maca, almonds, vanilla, sexy spices

1 ripe avocado, peeled and pitted, 2 cups frozen (preferably organic) blueberries, 2 t chia seeds, 6 Medjool dates, pitted, 2 T maca powder, 2 T raw almond butter, ½ t pure vanilla extract, 2 cups water, cinnamon, for sprinkling, pure maple syrup, for drizzling.

Place all ingredients in a blender and let sit for 30 minutes. Blend and pour into two bowls, sprinkle with cinnamon and drizzle with maple syrup.

If you happen to be an insomniac, regular romps under the covers are the best natural remedy for that much-needed shuteye.

Chapter 8

Exotic Spirits, Tonics & Elixirs

Gaia's Chocolate Mylk

This time around naptime is much more fun!

Sexy players: cacao, almonds, vanilla, maca

½ cup raw almonds, soaked for 2-3 hours

2 T coconut oil

4 T cacao powder

4 t maca powder

dash of cinnamon

4 T raw honey

¼ t pure vanilla extract

2 cups water

½ cup ice cubes

Peel and drain almonds. Place all ingredients in a blender and combine. Pour into two chilled mugs and sip with your sweetheart. Make love. Take a nap.

Inner Goddess HOT Cacao

Hot cacao is a sexual necessity during blustery winter months that chill you to the bone. Add spice variations that bring mindful delight to you and yours as you cuddle beneath the afghan.

Sexy players: dates, cacao, almonds, vanilla, maca, sexy spices

> **4 Medjool dates, pitted**
>
> **4 T cacao powder**
>
> **4 cups almond milk**
>
> **1 t pure vanilla extract**
>
> **2 t maca powder**
>
> **¼ t ground cinnamon**
>
> **1/8 t ground cayenne pepper**

Blend all sex – nourishing ingredients, then pour into a pot and set on fire! (or over medium-low heat) …

A poem begins as a lump in the throat, a sense of wrong, a homesickness, a lovesickness.

- Robert Frost

Essence of Rose Strawberry Nut Milk

Rose milk is a sensual delight hailing from southern India. Put on some exotic ragas and sip away 'til you and your loved one reach nirvana!

Sexy players: almonds, strawberries

30 almonds, soaked

2 cups almond milk

2 t pure maple syrup

2 t rose water

10 frozen strawberries

Soak almonds in water for 3-4 hours. Peel almonds and discard skins. Place all ingredients in a blender and blend until frothy. Pour into two chilled glasses.

Mystical Mylkshake of Saffron

If you have a tendency towards feeling blue, feeling fatigued, or simply desire an exotic dessert shake that won't keep you up all night, this one's for you. Love bonus: saffron is the queen of sexy spices.

Sexy players: almonds, dates, sexy spices

17 almonds, soaked in water for 2-3 hours, ½ t saffron threads, 4 Medjool dates, soaked for 2-3 hours, 2 cups almond milk, pinch turmeric, pinch cinnamon, ½ cup ice.

Soak almonds for 2-3 hours. Drain and peel almonds. Discard the peels. Soak dates for 2-3 hours and remove seeds. Soak saffron threads in the almond milk for 30 minutes to release sensual properties. Place all ingredients in a blender and blend until you have a frothy, creamy, luscious shake.

Saffron is the most expensive spice of them all. Grown in Iran, India and Spain, it is uplifting, mysterious and intoxicating. The delicate spice treats menstrual cramps, mild depression and insomnia. It rejuvenates the mind and is a potent aphrodisiac.

Anahita's Sharbat-e Tokhme Sharbati

Let Anahita, the Persian goddess of love pour you a glass of this traditional Iranian summer drink. Just letting the words sharbat-e tokhme sharbati spill from your mouth is sexy in itself, while chia seeds are the answer to sustaining sexual energy through steamy summer nights.

Sexy players: chia, citrus

4 t chia seeds

2 ½ cups cold water

2 T coconut sugar

½ cup warm water

1 T rose water

juice of 1 lemon or lime

Stir sugar into ½ cup warm water until it has dissolved fully. Stir chia seeds, dissolved sugar and water in a pitcher and let cool in fridge for two hours. Pour into two glasses. Add rose water and lemon or lime wedges. Sip with your lover.

To love another person is to see the face of God.   **– Victor Hugo**

Fragola's Bellini

Those Italians were on to something when they crafted this pretty little spirit. The Bellini was born in Venice, undoubtedly one of the sexiest spots on Earth.

Sexy players: strawberries, citrus

1 ripe peach, pitted and peeled

10 fragole (strawberries)

juice of 1 lime

club soda

champagne or Prosecco (as much as you like)

Blend peach, strawberries, lime juice and club soda to make a puree. Pour into two flutes and top with as much champagne or Prosecco as you like.

Sex must be mixed with tears, laughter, words, promises, scenes, jealousy, envy, all the spices of fear, foreign travel, new faces, novels, stories, dreams, fantasies, music, dancing, opium, wine.

- **Anais Nin**

Amazon Princess Martini

Martinis are one of the sexiest cocktails on Earth. A little spirit urges our sexual juices to flow. A lot of spirit dulls them. Drink in moderation for good prana to flow freely to your territories d'amour.

Sexy players: acai, citrus

2 T acai powder

4 oz. organic vodka

lots of honey or a little agave

nectar

juice of 2 lemons

In a cocktail shaker or glass, whisk the acai powder, honey and lemon juice. Let sit for fifteen minutes. Add vodka to the mix, shake and serve in Martini glasses, if you have them. If not, any vessel will do the trick.

You have to be very fond of men. Very, very fond. You have to be very fond of them to love them. Otherwise they're simply unbearable.

- Marguerite Duras

Lillet's Vodka Cocktail

I discovered Lillet Blanc on a warm summer evening at a café with my lover. A whimsical little French thing, it quickly became our favorite summer libation. A splash of organic vodka takes things up a notch, perfect if you only want one or two.

Sexy players: citrus

½ **cup Lillet Blanc**

½ **cup organic vodka**

¼ **cup freshly squeezed orange juice**

¼ **cup freshly squeezed lime juice**

ice

In a pitcher, stir together all ingredients, except ice. Pour into glasses, filled with ice and serve.

To get the full value of a joy, you must have someone to divide it with.

- Mark Twain

Chapter 9

Titillating Travel Snacks

Aphrodisical Cashews

Garam masala, the Indian spice mix featured here, contains many spices long revered for their aphrodisiac properties. Coriander is thought to heighten arousal for women. Fennel is a seed that increases sex drive in both sexes. Cloves boost energy and cinnamon increases blood flow. Keep these spicy love nuts with you in the car, on the train, on the boat or in the plane.

Sexy players: sexy spices

> **2 cups raw cashews**
>
> **2 T coconut oil**
>
> **1 t garam masala**
>
> **1 t sea salt**
>
> **¼ t cayenne pepper**
>
> **¼ t black pepper**

Roast cashew nuts in coconut oil over medium heat for 5 minutes. Transfer to a bowl and let cool. Meanwhile, combine all spices together in a small bowl. Sprinkle spices over nuts and stir.

Divinity's Date Bars

These dandy-licious energy bars spotlight the lusciously sensual date, considered to have a particularly strong aphrodisiac effect on the female species among us.

Sexy players: dates, almonds

> **1/4 cup chopped dates**
> **1/4 cup mixture dried cherries**
> **and goji berries**
> **1/3 raw mixed nuts (pistachios,**
> **cashews, almonds, Brazil nuts-**
> **you choose)**

Place dates and dried fruit in a food processor and grind until a paste forms. Remove and set in a bowl. Place nuts in food processor and process until chopped fine. Add nuts to fruit mixture and combine. Form into whatever shape you like and refrigerate for 2-3 hours.

What holds the world together, as I have learned from bitter experience, is sexual intercourse.

- Henry Miller

Aurora's Acai Truffles

Featured in these petit morsels of love is acai, that sexy siren who feeds our bodies with her divine antioxidant potency and amino acid power.

Sexy players: acai, maca, cacao, sexy spices, vanilla

¼ cup acai powder

2 T raw cacao powder

2 T raw almond butter

1 T raw honey

1 T coconut oil

10 Medjool dates, pitted

½ t sea salt

Place all ingredients in a food processor and combine until a dough forms. Roll the dough into rounds the size of your choice and place them in the refrigerator to sit for at least an hour.

A healthy libido decreases blood pressure, boosts the immune system and increases dopamine levels.

Sinfully Spiced Popcorn

Nutritional yeast, our charismatic lover, is a complete protein, containing 18 amino acids. Aside from these treats, add her to soups, stews and salads for enhanced sexual goodness.

Sexy players: nutritional yeast, sexy spices

½ cup popcorn kernels, 1/8 cup coconut oil, 1/8 cup nutritional yeast, 1 t garam masala, pinch cayenne pepper, sea salt, to taste.

Melt coconut oil and set aside. In an air-popper, pop the popcorn into a large bowl. Drizzle the coconut oil over the popcorn, coating as much as possible. In a small bowl combine the remaining ingredients. Sprinkle them in with the popcorn and combine thoroughly.

Protein is essential for a good sex life for many reasons. Your neurotransmitters (brain chemicals responsible for sexual urges) are made of protein and need it to effectively communicate with each other.

Sexy Spicy Maca Balls

Maca is a natural root from Peru with a long history as a sex enhancer. It also increases strength, stamina, energy, fertility and libido.

Sexy players: almonds, maca, cacao, sexy spices, vanilla

¼ cup raw almond butter

1 T maca powder

1 T raw cacao powder

dash cayenne pepper

splash pure vanilla extract

drop of raw honey

Place all ingredients in your food processor. Combine. Form dough into balls the size of your liking. Store in the fridge for at least 30 minutes, or as long as you like. These are treats with minimal mess – best taken to the bedroom for eating and other experiments.

He who wants a rose, must respect her thorn.

- Andre Gide

Killing Me Softly Kale Chips

If you eat a bit of kale daily, your sex drive
will smile on you with ease and inner calm.

Sexy players: leafy greens, nutritional
yeast, sexy spices

**6 cups kale leaves, cleaned
2 T extra-virgin, unrefined
coconut oil, melted
4 T nutritional yeast
¼ t cayenne pepper
¼ t garam masala
generous pinch of sea salt
pinch of ground black
pepper**

Preheat oven to 350 degrees. On a baking
sheet, toss kale with coconut oil and
seasonings. Bake for 10-15 minutes,
depending upon the strength of your oven.
Place in a large bowl and eat with your mitts.

**For I have learned that every heart will
get what it prays for most.**
                                    - Hafiz

Take Me With You Acai Energy Bars

A change of scenery can supercharge your sex life when the daily grind fails to. If you're in the mood to pack your partner and venture off into the wild blue yonder, you'll want to pack an ample supply of these super sexy treats.

Sexy players: dates, acai, almonds, vanilla, sexy spices

12 Medjool dates, pitted

4 T acai powder

1 cup dried pineapple pieces

1 cup raw cashews

1 ½ cups raw almonds

1 t pure vanilla extract

½ t ground cinnamon

dash of sea salt

Process all ingredients until they are fully combined. Place mixture on a baking sheet lined with Saran wrap. Mold it into a rectangle. Cover with Saran wrap and let sit in refrigerator for upwards of one hour. Cut into small squares and nibble with pleasure as you travel.

Acai Amour Cacao Macaroons

These tasty little treats will make you feel like you're nibbling in the French Tropics. With the blend of acai, cacao, vanilla and maca, you've got a recipe for sexual success.

Sexy players: cacao, acai, vanilla, maca

> **1 ½ cups unsweetened, shredded coconut, ¾ cup raw cacao powder, ½ cup raw agave or honey, 1 T coconut oil, melted, 2 T acai powder, ¼ t pure vanilla extract, ½ t sea salt, 2 T maca powder.**

In a large bowl, stir all ingredients together. Scoop tablespoon-sized rounds of the batter onto a tray and place in freezer. Let sit for 30 minutes. Feed these bite-sized morsels to the one you adore.

Even when she walks, one would believe that she dances.

- Charles Baudelaire

Beloved Bars of Strawberries & Dates

Travel with these to your office, your garden, to the oceans, to the mountains, but offer them first to your beloved. The rewards will be many.

Sexy players: dates, oats, vanilla, sexy spices, strawberries

> 1 cup pitted Medjool dates
> 1/4 cup raw cashews
> 2 heaping T rolled oats
> 1 t pure vanilla extract
> 1/4 t cinnamon
> 1/4 t sea salt
> 1 cup organic strawberries, sliced thin

Place dates, cashews, oats, vanilla, cinnamon and sea salt in a food processor. Pulse until well-combined.
Press the date mixture into the bottom of a pan and top with strawberries. Cut into squares or triangles and serve or refrigerate. Will keep in the fridge for a few days.

When someone shows you who they are, believe them.

- Maya Angelou

Give it to me Raw, Brownies

These are the perfect little treats to enjoy while being tied up, (perhaps to a terribly luxurious 4 - poster bed?) You may find your taste buds responding in a heightened fashion while being fed and lightly bitten.

Sexy players: dates, almonds, cacao, vanilla

1 cup Medjool dates, pitted and soaked

1 cup raw almonds

2 T raw cacao powder

1 t pure vanilla extract

a large pinch of sea salt

a splash of maple syrup, as needed for binding

In a food processor or high-speed blender, start processing the almonds and sea salt. When they turn into miniscule morsels, add in the dates, cacao powder and vanilla. Continue to mix until a dough-like consistency forms, adding maple syrup as needed. Shape the dough into little squares and refrigerate. Save for later or eat them now if you're ready to get busy in the sac.

To love or have loved, that is enough.
Ask nothing further. There is no other
pearl to be found in the dark folds of life.

- Victor Hugo

Gratitude

Thank you for reading and supporting this sexy vegan project. I hope you all have loads of fun experimenting in the kitchen and the bedroom - with the **sexy players** and your **sexy paramours**. Here's to wearing your loving hearts on your sleeves, exploring transcendental flavors of sexual union & making memorable, moveable feasts!

If you have any thoughts for me, please send your musings to: sexyvegankitchen@gmail.com or leave a kind word or two (or three) at the sexy vegan blog: http://theglobalvegan.blogspot.com

Merci & Bon Chance!

- Aimee

ABOUT THE AUTHOR

Aimee Christine Hughes is a health and wellness expert, yoga devotee and seasoned traveler. She contributes regular articles to Nature & Health magazine, Australia's leading wellness publication and On Fitness magazine, a publication dedicated to fitness and natural health. She has written for Reader's Digest (Canada), E/The Environmental Magazine, Elephant Journal, Living Green Magazine, Alive (Canada), Traveller magazine (U.K.), Go World Travel, The South China Morning Post, (Hong Kong) and many others. This is her first book.

~ Just a few additional pages for your own personal musings (optional) ~ xo

Made in the USA
Charleston, SC
01 July 2013